The Early Years
A Charlotte Mason Preschool Handbook

by
Karen Smith and Sonya Shafer

The Early Years: A Charlotte Mason Preschool Handbook
© 2009, Karen Smith and Sonya Shafer

All rights reserved. No part of this work may be reproduced or distributed in any form by any means—graphic, electronic, or mechanical, including photocopying, recording, taping, or storing in information storage and retrieval systems—without written permission from the publisher.

ISBN: 978-1-61634-071-1

Cover Design: John Shafer

Published by
Simply Charlotte Mason, LLC
P.O. Box 892
Grayson, Georgia 30017-0892

www.SimplyCharlotteMason.com

Contents

The Early Years 5
Introduction 7

Part 1: The Chief Duty of Parents

Chapter 1: A Parent's Chief Duty 11

Part 2: Form Right Habits of Thinking and Behaving

Chapter 2: Proper Physical Care 19
Chapter 3: Habit Training 27

Part 3: Nourish the Mind on Loving, Right, and Noble Ideas

Chapter 4: Using the Senses 45
Chapter 5: Outdoor Life 55
Chapter 6: Personal Acquaintance with Nature 71
Chapter 7: Play 81
Chapter 8: Books & Stories 83
Chapter 9: Language 89
Chapter 10: Music & Art 93
Chapter 11: Spiritual Life 97
Chapter 12: The Alphabet 111
Chapter 13: A Gifted Child 115

Appendix
Charlotte's Thoughts on Kindergarten 121
Beginning Reading 130
Math Concepts 141
Handwriting 142

The Early Years

"To form in his child right habits of thinking and behaving is a parent's chief duty, . . . To nourish a child daily with loving, right, and noble ideas we believe to be the parent's next duty" (Vol. 2, p. 228).

Introduction

Being a mother of a preschooler (or several preschoolers) can be a challenge. Probably no other season of life is so demanding. It's no wonder that a young mother is often worn-out, exhausted, and bewildered. Believe us, we know. We've been there eight times.

Voices come at you from all sides, telling you what you should be doing with those little children. Just when you think you're doing a pretty good job, someone criticizes the path you have chosen and adds "new and improved" information that makes you feel like a bad mommy. Pressure mounts as "experts" and relatives shake their heads and unroll a list of expectations before your weary eyes.

Relax. Take a deep breath. The counsel you will find in these pages is unlike those others. The early years are not years for high pressure or organized activities with a tight schedule. Nor are they years for stuffing your child's head full of facts. You don't even have to buy craft supplies!

Charlotte Mason's counsel to mothers of preschoolers is clearly sensible, easily doable, and utterly refreshing. Charlotte's comments will give you permission to step off the whirling merry-go-round of activities, academics, and stress, and step into a peaceful world of simplicity, good old-fashioned fun, and sanity again.

Enjoy the early years!

Excerpts from Charlotte Mason's books are surrounded by quotation marks and accompanied by a reference to which book in the series the excerpt came from.
- Vol. 1: Home Education
- Vol. 2: Parents and Children
- Vol. 3: School Education
- Vol. 4: Ourselves
- Vol. 5: Formation of Character
- Vol. 6: A Philosophy of Education

Comments or suggestions that have been added by the authors of this book are not in quotation marks and have no reference.

Part 1

The Chief Duty of Parents

Chapter 1
A Parent's Chief Duty

Charlotte believed that parents have two duties to focus on as they raise and educate their children. Those two duties are to form in your child right habits of thinking and behaving, and to nourish your child's mind with loving, right, and noble ideas. Here are some of her practical reminders about those two duties. In the rest of this book, we'll look at specific activities you can use to form good habits and provide right ideas.

Charlotte's Thoughts on A Parent's Chief Duty

1. Understand that bringing up and educating your child is the most important job in society.

"Now, that work which is of most importance to society is the bringing-up and instruction of the children—in the school, certainly, but far more in the home, because it is more than anything else the home influences brought to bear upon the child that determine the character and career of the future man or woman" (Vol. 1, p. 1).

2. Form in your child right habits of thinking and behaving.

"To form in his child right habits of thinking and behaving is a parent's chief duty" (Vol. 2, p. 228).

"By *'education is a discipline,'* we mean the discipline of habits, formed definitely and thoughtfully, whether habits of mind or body" (Vol. 6, Preface).

3. Nourish your child's mind with loving, right, and noble ideas.

"To nourish a child daily with loving, right, and noble ideas we believe to be the parent's next duty" (Vol. 2, p. 228).

"Now that life, which we call education, receives only one kind of sustenance; it grows upon *ideas*." (Vol. 2, p. 33).

"The duty of parents is to sustain a child's inner life with ideas as they sustain his body with food" (Vol. 2, p. 39).

"The child has affinities with evil as well as with good; therefore, hedge him about from any chance lodgment of evil ideas" (Vol. 2, p. 39).

"In saying that *'education is a life,'* the need of intellectual and moral as well as of physical sustenance is implied. The mind feeds on ideas, and therefore children should have a generous curriculum" (Vol. 6, Preface).

Notes

Keep in mind that to "educate" means to help form a child's mind, character, or physical ability. Education encompasses all that you do to cultivate, nourish, and train your child as a person.

"To form in his child right habits of thinking and behaving is a parent's chief duty."

Notes

"In the early days of a child's life it makes little apparent difference whether we educate with a notion of filling a receptacle, inscribing a tablet, moulding plastic matter, or nourishing a life, but as a child grows we shall perceive that only those *ideas* which have fed his life, are taken into his being; all the rest is cast away or is, like sawdust in the system, an impediment and an injury" (Vol. 6, pp. 108, 109).

4. Make sure everything you give your child is wholesome and nourishing, including the atmosphere in which he grows.

"The parents' chief care is, that that which they supply shall be wholesome and nourishing, whether in the way of picture-books, lessons, playmates, bread and milk, or mother's love" (Vol. 1, p. 5).

"Every look of gentleness and tone of reverence, every word of kindness and act of help, passes into the thought-environment, the very atmosphere which the child breathes; he does not think of these things, may never think of them, but all his life long they excite that 'vague appetency towards something' out of which most of his actions spring. Oh, wonderful and dreadful presence of the little child in the midst! "That he should take direction and inspiration from all the casual life about him, should make our poor words and ways the starting-point from which, and in the direction of which, he develops—this is a thought which makes the best of us hold our breath. There is no way of escape for parents; they must needs be as 'inspirers' to their children, because about them hangs, as its atmosphere about a planet, the thought-environment of the child, from which he derives those enduring ideas which express themselves as a life-long 'appetency' towards things sordid or things lovely, things earthly or divine" (Vol. 2, pp. 36, 37).

5. Trust your personal insights into your child, but also continue to educate yourself as a parent.

"Allow me to say once more, that I venture to write upon subjects bearing on home education with the greatest deference to mothers; believing, that in virtue of their peculiar insight into the dispositions of their own children, they are blest with both knowledge and power in the management of them which lookers-on can only admire from afar. At the same time, there is such a thing as a *science* of education, that does not come by intuition, in the knowledge of which it is possible to bring up a child entirely according to natural law, which is also Divine law, in the keeping of which there is great reward" (Vol. 1, p. 135).

6. Remember that educating your child as a whole person requires flexibility as you deal with each unique individual.

"The central thought, or rather body of thought, upon which I found, is the somewhat obvious fact that the child is a *person* with all the possibilities and powers included in personality" (Vol. 1, Preface).

"Parents are very jealous over the individuality of their children; they mistrust the tendency to develop all on the same plan; and this instinctive jealousy is right; for, supposing that education really did consist in systematised efforts to draw out every power that is in us, why, we should all develop on the same lines, be as like as 'two peas,' and (should we not?) die of weariness of one another!" (Vol. 2, p. 31).

> "To nourish a child daily with loving, right, and noble ideas we believe to be the parent's next duty."

"We believe that children are human beings at their best and sweetest, but also at their weakest and least wise. We are careful not to dilute life for them, but to present such portions to them in such quantities as they can readily receive" (Vol. 2, p. 232).

7. Give your child a natural home atmosphere in which to learn, rather than in a contrived "child environment."

"When we say that *'education is an atmosphere,'* we do not mean that a child should be isolated in what may be called a 'child-environment' especially adapted and prepared, but that we should take into account the educational value of his natural home atmosphere, both as regards persons and things, and should let him live freely among his proper conditions. It stultifies a child to bring down his world to the 'child's' level" (Vol. 6, Preface).

"It is not an environment that these want, a set of artificial relations carefully constructed, but an *atmosphere* which nobody has been at pains to constitute. It is there, about the child, his natural element, precisely as the atmosphere of the earth is about us. It is thrown off, as it were, from persons and things, stirred by events, sweetened by love, ventilated, kept in motion, by the regulated action of common sense. We all know the natural conditions under which a child should live; how he shares household ways with his mother, romps with his father, is teased by his brothers and petted by his sisters; is taught by his tumbles; learns self-denial by the baby's needs, the delightfulness of furniture by playing at battle and siege with sofa and table; learns veneration for the old by the visits of his great-grandmother; how to live with his equals by the chums he gathers round him; learns intimacy with animals from his dog and cat; delight in the fields where the buttercups grow and greater delight in the blackberry hedges. And, what tempered 'fusion of classes' is so effective as a child's intimacy with his betters, and also with cook and housemaid, blacksmith and joiner, with everybody who comes in his way? Children have a genius for this sort of general intimacy, a valuable part of their education; care and guidance are needed, of course, lest admiring friends should make fools of them, but no compounded 'environment' could make up for this fresh air, this wholesome wind blowing now from one point, now from another" (Vol. 6, pp. 96, 97).

8. Consider postponing formal school lessons until your child is six.

"We (of the P.N.E.U.) begin the definite 'school' education of children when they are six; they are no doubt capable of beginning a year or two earlier but the fact is that nature and circumstances have provided such a wide field of education for young children that it seems better to abstain from requiring *direct* intellectual efforts until they have arrived at that age" (Vol. 6, p. 159).

9. Remember that your child is learning by leaps and bounds during his early years, simply from observing and interacting with everything around him.

"Does the child eat or drink, does he come, or go, or play—all the time he is being educated, though he is as little aware of it as he is of the act of breathing" (Vol. 1, p. 8).

"Let us consider, in the first two years of life they manage to get through more

---

Notes

Read Charlotte's thoughts on Kindergarten on pages 121–129.

P.N.E.U. stands for Parents' National Education Union, an organization that Charlotte founded based on her methods and philosophy.

"Does the child eat or drink, does he come, or go, or play—all the time he is being educated."

Notes

An Early Years Guide that reinforces the concepts in this book is provided free at http://SimplyCharlotteMason.com/planning/eyguide/

intellectual effort than any following two years can show. Supposing that much-discussed Martian were at last able to make his way to our planet, think of how much he must learn before he could accommodate himself to our conditions! Our notions of hard and soft, wet and dry, hot and cold, stable and unstable, far and near, would be as foreign to him as they are to an infant who holds out his pinafore for the moon. We do not know what the Martian means of locomotion are but we can realise that to run and jump and climb stairs, even to sit and stand at will must require fully as much reasoned endeavour as it takes in after years to accomplish skating, dancing, ski-ing, fencing, whatever athletic exercises people spend years in perfecting; and all these the infant accomplishes in his first two years. He learns the properties of matter, knows colours and has first notions of size, solid, liquid; has learned in his third year to articulate with surprising clearness. What is more, he has learned a language, two languages, if he has had the opportunity, and the writer has known of three languages being mastered by a child of three, and one of them was Arabic; mastered, that is, so far that a child can say all that he needs to say in any one of the three—the sort of mastery most of us wish for when we are travelling in foreign countries" (Vol. 6, p. 35).

"He is engaged in self-education, taking his lessons from everything he sees and hears, and strengthening his powers by everything he does" (Vol. 6, pp. 37, 38).

"But we forget that the child has inborn cravings after all we have given him. Just as the healthy child must have his dinner and his bed, so too does he crave for knowledge, perfection, beauty, power, society; and all he wants is opportunity. Give him opportunities of loving and learning, and he will love and learn, for ''tis his nature to.' Whoever has taken note of the sweet reasonableness, the quick intelligence, the bright imaginings of a child, will think the fuss we make about the right studies for developing these is like asking, How shall we get a hungry man to eat his dinner?" (Vol. 2, p. 70).

Questions to Ask about A Parent's Chief Duty

- Do I truly believe that my job as a parent is important?
- Am I seeking to instill in my child right habits of thinking and behaving?
- Am I trying to nourish my child's mind with loving, right, and noble ideas?
- Am I being careful to give my child only what is wholesome and nourishing?
- Am I continuing to educate myself in order to grow as a parent?
- Am I treating each child as a unique individual and staying flexible?
- Am I allowing my child to grow up in a natural home environment?
- Am I comfortable with postponing formal academic lessons until my child is six?
- Do I believe that my child is growing in many ways simply by observing and interacting with his surroundings?

"He is engaged in self-education, taking his lessons from everything he sees and hears."

More Quotes on A Parent's Chief Duty

"No man should bring children into the world who is unwilling to persevere to the end in their nature and education."—Plato

"To educate a man in mind and not in morals is to educate a menace to society."—Theodore Roosevelt

"A mind once stretched by a new idea never regains its original dimension."—Oliver Wendell Holmes

---

Notes

"Give him opportunities of loving and learning, and he will love and learn."

Part 2

Form Right Habits of Thinking and Behaving

Chapter 2
Proper Physical Care

"Sometimes I feel like all I do is change diapers, cook food, and clean up messes," sighed Ann.

Glenda smiled. "I remember those days well," she replied. "It is a hard season of life, but I want you to think about how important those tasks are, dear."

"Oh, I don't know about that," said Ann. "They certainly don't feel important. Now, reading a book together or teaching Troy a new word—those feel important."

"Do you remember when Tim and I went on that trip last summer?" Glenda asked, "I'll never forget the sight of those children in that orphanage. There were so many of them, and so few helpers, that those basic necessary tasks didn't get done. There was no one to change their messy diapers, no one to feed them when they were hungry, and no one to clean. Dirt was everywhere." Glenda looked into Ann's eyes. "You are ministering to your children, Ann. You are nourishing their spirits just as much as you are caring for their physical bodies. I know it doesn't feel important sometimes, but let me assure you that it is one of the most important areas of ministry that you will ever have. Thank you for being faithful to take care of your children's needs."

Little Troy appeared in the doorway, rubbing the afternoon sleep from his eyes. "I'm hungry, Mommy. And Sammy has a stinky diaper."

Ann smiled as she opened her arms wide for an after-nap hug.

Charlotte's Thoughts on Proper Physical Care

1. Don't hinder his physical well-being.

"She [the mother] may cast a stumbling-block in the way of physical life by giving him unwholesome food, letting him sleep and live in ill-ventilated rooms, by disregarding any or every of the simple laws of health, ignorance of which is hardly to be excused in the face of the pains taken by scientific men to bring this necessary knowledge within the reach of every one" (Vol. 1, p. 16).

"Neither is it lawful for parents to impose any unnecessary rigours upon their children; this was the error of the eighteenth century and of the early decades of our own age, when hunger, cold, and denial, which was by no means self-denial, were supposed wholesome for children" (Vol. 3, pp. 103, 104).

2. Have a physical, as well as character, ideal in mind.

"The child is born with certain natural tendencies, and, according to his bringing-up, each such tendency may run into a blemish of person or character, or into a cognate grace. Therefore, it is worth while to have even a *physical* ideal for one's child; not, for instance, to be run away with by the notion that a fat child is necessarily a fine child. The fat child can easily be produced: but the bright eyes, the open regard, the springing step; the tones, clear as a bell; the agile, graceful

"The agile, graceful movements that characterise the well-brought-up child, are the result, not of bodily well-being only, but of 'mind and soul according well,' of a quick, trained intelligence, and of a moral nature habituated to the 'joy of self control.'"

movements that characterise the well-brought-up child, are the result, not of bodily well-being only, but of 'mind and soul according well,' of a quick, trained intelligence, and of a moral nature habituated to the 'joy of self control' " (Vol. 1, p. 95).

3. Keep in mind that physical health can have a direct influence on intellectual, moral, and even spiritual growth.

"I fear the reader may be inclined to think that I am inviting his attention for the most part to a few physiological matters—the lowest round of the educational ladder. The lowest round it may be, but yet it *is* the lowest round, the necessary step to all the rest. For it is not too much to say that, in our present state of being, intellectual, moral, even spiritual life and progress depend greatly upon physical conditions. That is to say, not that he who has a fine physique is necessarily a good and clever man; but that the good and clever man requires much animal substance to make up for the expenditure of tissue brought about in the exercise of his virtue and his intellect. For example, is it easier to be amiable, kindly, candid, with or without a headache or an attack of neuralgia?" (Vol. 1, p. 37).

Meals

1. Good nutrition can affect your child's brain as well as body.

"The brain cannot do its work well unless it be abundantly and suitably nourished; somebody has made a calculation of how many ounces of brain went to the production of such a work—say *Paradise Lost*—how many to such another, and so on. Without going into mental arithmetic of this nature, we may say with safety that every sort of intellectual activity wastes the tissues of the brain; a network of vessels supplies an enormous quantity of blood to the organ, to make up for this waste of material; and the vigour and health of the brain depend upon the quality and quantity of this blood-supply.

"Now, the quality of the blood is affected by three or four causes. In the first place, the blood is elaborated from the food; the more nutritious and easy of digestion the food, the more *vital* will be the properties of the blood" (Vol. 1, pp. 24, 25).

2. Give your child a variety of healthful foods to help nourish his brain and replenish his body cells.

"The food must be varied, too, a mixed diet, because various ingredients are required to make up for the various waste in the tissues. The children are shocking spendthrifts; their endless goings and comings, their restlessness, their energy, the very wagging of their tongues, all mean expenditure of substance: the loss is not appreciable, but they lose something by every sudden sally, out of doors or within. No doubt the gain of power which results from exercise is more than compensation for the loss of substance; but, all the same, this loss must be promptly made good. And not only is the body of the child more active, proportionably, than that of the man: the child's brain as compared with a man's is in a perpetual flutter of endeavour. It is calculated that though the brain of a man weighs no more than a fortieth part of his body, yet a fifth or sixth of his whole complement of blood

> "Even for tea and breakfast the wise mother does not say, 'I always give my children' so and so."

goes to nourish this delicate and intensely active organ; but, in the child's case, a considerably larger proportion of the blood that is in him is spent on the sustenance of his brain. And all the time, with these excessive demands upon him, the child has to grow! not merely to make up for waste, but to produce new substance in brain and body" (Vol. 1, p. 25).

"But, given pleasant surroundings and excellent food, and even then the requirements of these exacting little people are not fully met: plain as their food should be, they must have variety. A leg of mutton every Tuesday, the same cold on Wednesday, and hashed on Thursday, may be very good food; but the child who has this diet week after week is inadequately nourished, simply because he is tired of it. The mother should contrive a rotation for her children that will last at least a fortnight, without the same dinner recurring twice. Fish, especially if the children dine off it without meat to follow, is excellent as a change, the more so as it is rich in phosphorus—a valuable brain food. The children's puddings deserve a good deal of consideration, because they do not commonly care for fatty foods, but prefer to derive the warmth of their bodies from the starch and sugar of their puddings. But give them a variety; do not let it be 'everlasting tapioca.' Even for tea and breakfast the wise mother does not say, 'I always give my children' so and so. They should not have anything 'always'; every meal should have some little surprise. But is this the way, to make them think overmuch of what they shall eat and drink? On the contrary, it is the underfed children who are greedy, and unfit to be trusted with any unusual delicacy" (Vol. 1, pp. 27, 28).

3. Give your child enough food to help him grow and flourish both physically and mentally.

"The child must be well fed. Half the people of low vitality we come across are the victims of low-feeding during their childhood; and that more often because their parents were not alive to their duty in this respect, then because they were not in a position to afford their children the diet necessary to their full physical and mental development" (Vol. 1, pp. 25, 26).

4. Eat regular meals at usual intervals throughout the day.

"Regular meals at, usually, *unbroken* intervals—dinner, never more than five hours after breakfast; luncheon, unnecessary; animal food, once certainly, in some lighter form, twice a day—are the suggestions of common sense followed out in most well-regulated households" (Vol. 1, p. 26).

5. Limit rich or fried foods and make sure your child drinks enough water.

"But it is not the food which is *eaten*, but the food which is *digested*, that nourishes body and brain. And here so many considerations press, that we can only glance at two or three of the most obvious. Everybody knows that children should not eat pastry, or pork, or fried meats, or cheese, or rich, highly-flavoured food of any description; that pepper, mustard, and vinegar, sauces and spices, should be forbidden, with new bread, rich cakes, and jams, like plum or gooseberry, in which the leathery coat of the fruit is preserved; that milk, or milk and water, and that not too warm, or cocoa, is the best drink for children, and that they should be trained not to drink until they have finished eating; that fresh fruit at breakfast is

Notes

Though some details may have changed since Charlotte lived, the principles of healthy eating remain.

"Regular meals at, usually, *unbroken* intervals."

invaluable; that, as serving the same end, oatmeal porridge and treacle, and the fat of toasted bacon, are valuable breakfast foods; and that a glass of water, also, taken the last thing at night and the first thing in the morning, is useful in promoting those regular habits on which much of the comfort of life depends" (Vol. 1, p. 26).

6. Keep meal times pleasant.

"Again let me say, it is *digested* food that nourishes the system, and people are apt to forget how far mental and moral conditions affect the processes of digestion. The fact is, that the gastric juices which act as solvents to the viands are only secreted freely when the mind is in a cheerful and contented frame. If the child dislike his dinner, he swallows it, but the digestion of that distasteful meal is a laborious, much-impeded process: if the meal be eaten in silence, unrelieved by pleasant chat, the child loses much of the 'good' of his dinner. Hence it is not a matter of pampering them at all, but a matter of health, of due nutrition, that the children should enjoy their food, and that their meals should be eaten in gladness; though, by the way, joyful *excitement* is as mischievous as its opposite in destroying that even, cheerful tenor of mind favourable to the processes of digestion. No pains should be spared to make the hours of meeting round the family table the brightest hours of the day. This is supposing that the children are allowed to sit at the same table with their parents; and, if it is possible to let them do so at every meal excepting a late dinner, the advantage to the little people is incalculable" (Vol. 1, pp. 26, 27).

7. Use meal times to practice good manners and reinforce good habits.

"Here is the parents' opportunity to train them in manners and morals, to cement family love, and to accustom the children to habits, such as that of thorough mastication, for instance, as important on the score of health as on that of propriety" (Vol. 1, p. 27).

Appropriate Clothing & Hygiene

1. Remember that perspiration is a natural and helpful function of the body.

"If the brain is to be duly nourished, it is important to keep the whole surface of the skin in a condition to throw off freely the excretions of the blood [perspiration]" (Vol. 1, p. 36).

2. Regular baths help remove dead cells and dirt from the skin's surface.

"Two considerations follow: of the first, the necessity for the daily bath, followed by vigorous rubbing of the skin, it is needless to say a word here" (Vol. 1, p. 36).

3. Make sure your child wears clothing that is porous enough to allow free perspiration.

"But possibly it is not so well understood that children should be clothed in porous garments which admit of the instant passing off of the exhalations of the skin. Why did delicate women faint, or, at any rate, 'feel faint,' when it was the custom to go to church in sealskin coats? Why do people who sleep under down, or even under silk or cotton quilts, frequently rise unrefreshed? From the one cause: their coverings have impeded the passage of the insensible [not felt with the senses] perspiration, and so have hindered the skin in its function of relieving the blood of impurities. It is surprising what a constant loss of vitality many people experience from no other cause than the unsuitable character of their clothing" (Vol. 1, p. 36).

Fresh Air & Exercise

1. Remember that fresh air is as important as healthful food to nourish the brain.

"The quality of the blood depends almost as much on the air we breathe as on the food we eat; in the course of every two or three minutes, all the blood in the body passes through the endless ramifications of the lungs, for no other purpose than that, during the instant of its passage, it should be acted upon by the oxygen contained in the air which is drawn into the lungs in the act of breathing. But what can happen to the blood in the course of an exposure of so short duration? Just this—the whole character, the very colour, of the blood is changed: it enters the lungs spoiled, no longer capable of sustaining life; it leaves them, a pure and vital fluid. Now, observe, the blood is only fully oxygenated when the air contains its full proportion of oxygen, and every breathing and burning object withdraws some oxygen from the atmosphere. Hence the importance of giving the children daily airings and abundant exercise of limb and lung in unvitiated, unimpoverished air" (Vol. 1, pp. 28, 29).

2. A daily "constitutional" walk is not the best solution, though it is better than nothing.

" 'The children walk every day; they are never out less than an hour when the weather is suitable.' That is better than nothing; so is this:—An East London schoolmistress notices the pale looks of one of her best girls. 'Have you had any dinner, Nellie?' 'Ye-es' (with hesitation). 'What have you had?' 'Mother gave Jessie and me a halfpenny to buy our dinners, and we bought a haporth of aniseed drops—they go further than bread'—with an appeal in her eyes against possible censure for extravagance. Children do not develop at their best upon aniseed drops for dinner, nor upon an hour's 'constitutional' daily" (Vol. 1, p. 29).

3. Keep the house well ventilated to replenish the supply of oxygen-rich air.

"We know all about it; what we forget, perhaps, is, that even oxygen has its limitation: nothing can act but where it is, and, waste attends work, hold true for this vital gas as for other matters. Fire and lamp and breathing beings are all consumers of the oxygen which sustains them. What follows? Why, that this element, which is present in the ration of twenty-three parts to the hundred in pure air, is subject to an enormous drain within the four walls of a house, where the air is more or less stationary" (Vol. 1, pp. 30, 31).

"About out-of-door airings we shall have occasion to speak more fully; but *indoor* airings are truly as important, because, if the tissues be nourished upon impure blood for all the hours the child spends in the house, the mischief will not

Notes

Charlotte favored wool for this porous clothing. "The children cannot be better dressed throughout than in loosely woven woollen garments, flannels and serges, of varying thicknesses for summer and winter wear. Woollens have other advantages over cotton and linen materials besides that of being porous. Wool is a bad conductor, and therefore does not allow of the too free escape of the animal heat; and it is absorbent, and therefore relieves the skin of the clammy sensations which follow sensible [felt by the senses] perspiration. We should be the better for it if we could make up our minds to sleep in wool, discarding linen or cotton in favour of sheets made of some lightly woven woollen material" (Vol. 1, pp. 36, 37).

"Children do not develop at their best upon aniseed drops for dinner, nor upon an hour's 'constitutional' daily."

be mended in the shorter intervals spent out of doors. Put two or three breathing bodies, as well as fire and gas, into a room, and it is incredible how soon the air becomes vitiated unless it be constantly renewed; that is, unless the room be well ventilated. We know what is to come in out of the fresh air and complain that a room feels stuffy; but sit in the room a few minutes, and you get accustomed to its stuffiness; the senses are no longer a safe guide.

"Therefore, regular provision must be made for the ventilation of rooms regardless of the feelings of their inmates; *at least* an inch of window open at the top, day and night, renders a room tolerably safe, because it allows the escape of the vitiated air, which, being light, ascends, leaving room for the influx of colder, fresher air by cracks and crannies in doors and floors. An open chimney is a useful, though not a sufficient, ventilator; it is needless to say that the stopping-up of chimneys in sleeping-rooms is suicidal. It is particularly important to accustom children to sleep with an inch or two, or more, of open window all through the year—as much more as you like in the summer" (Vol. 1, pp. 33, 34).

"When the children are out of a room which they commonly occupy, day nursery or breakfast room, then is the opportunity to air it thoroughly by throwing windows and doors wide open and producing a thorough draught" (Vol. 1, p. 34).

4. Spend time outside in the fresh air as much as possible.

"True, we must needs have houses for shelter from the weather by day and for rest at night; but in proportion as we cease to make our houses 'comfortable,' as we regard them merely as necessary shelters when we cannot be out of doors, shall we enjoy to the full the vigorous vitality possible to us" (Vol. 1, p. 31).

5. Allow your child to enjoy the sunshine, both indoors and out.

"Now, it is observed that people who live much in the sunshine are of a ruddy countenance—that is, a great many of these red corpuscles are present in their blood; while the poor souls who live in cellars and sunless alleys have skins the colour of whity-brown paper. Therefore, it is concluded that light and sunshine are favourable to the production of red corpuscles in the blood; and, *therefore*—to this next 'therefore' is but a step for the mother—the children's rooms should be on the sunny side of the house, with a south aspect if possible. Indeed, the whole house should be kept light and bright for their sakes; trees and outbuildings that obstruct the sunshine and make the children's rooms dull should be removed without hesitation" (Vol. 1, pp. 34, 35).

"They want light, solar light, as well as air. Country people are ruddier than town folk; miners are sallow, so are the dwellers in cellars and in sunless valleys. The reason is, that, to secure the ruddy glow of perfect health, certain changes must take place in the blood—the nature of which it would take too long to explain here—and that these changes in the blood, marked by the free production of red corpuscles, appear to take place most favourably under the influence of abundant solar light" (Vol. 1, p. 94).

Notes

See also chapter 5, Outdoor Life.

Regular moderate exposure to sunshine helps the body manufacture vitamin D.

"In proportion as we cease to make our houses 'comfortable,' as we regard them merely as necessary shelters when we cannot be out of doors, shall we enjoy to the full the vigorous vitality possible to us."

6. Daily physical exercise can benefit your child both physically and mentally.

"To give the child pleasure in light and easy motion—the sort of delight in the management of his own body that a good rider finds in managing his horse—dancing, drill, calisthenics, some sort of judicious physical exercise, should make part of every day's routine. Swedish drill is especially valuable, and many of the exercises are quite suitable for the nursery. Certain moral qualities come into play in alert movements, eye-to-eye attention, prompt and intelligent replies; but it often happens that good children fail in these points for want of physical training" (Vol. 1, p. 132).

Questions to Ask about Proper Physical Care

- Am I being careful not to hinder my child's physical well-being?
- Do I have a healthy and realistic physical ideal in mind for my child, as well as a character ideal?
- Do I understand how my child's physical well-being can have an impact on his intellectual, moral, and spiritual growth?
- Do I understand how good nutrition can affect my child's brain as well as his body?
- Am I trying to give my child a variety of healthful foods?
- Am I seeking to give my child enough food to help him grow and flourish physically and mentally?
- Do we normally eat regular meals at usual intervals throughout the day?
- Do I try to limit rich or fried foods, and do I try to make sure my child drinks plenty of water?
- Am I doing what I can to keep meal times pleasant?
- Am I trying to use meal times to practice good manners and reinforce good habits?
- Do I understand that perspiration is natural and helpful?
- Do I give my child regular baths?
- Am I careful to dress my child in comfortable, porous clothing that will allow him to play and perspire?
- Do I understand that fresh air is as important to the brain as nutritious food?
- Am I satisfied with a daily "constitutional" walk, or could I do more to help my child breathe fresh air?
- Am I trying to keep the house well ventilated?
- Am I trying to spend lots of time outside in the fresh air?
- Do I encourage my child to enjoy the sunshine?
- Am I seeking to give my child daily physical exercise?

More Quotes about Proper Physical Care

"Better is a dinner of herbs where love is, than a stalled ox and hatred therewith."—Proverbs 15:17

Notes

Swedish Drill was similar to an advanced sort of Simon Says. You can download a free book about Swedish Drill at http://SimplyCharlotteMason.com/books/swedish-drill-teacher/

"Dancing, drill, calisthenics, some sort of judicious physical exercise, should make part of every day's routine."

Notes

"Water, air, and cleanness are the chief articles in my pharmacy."—Napoleon Bonaparte

"If we could give every individual the right amount of nourishment and exercise, not too little and not too much, we would have found the safest way to health."—Hippocrates

"There was never a child so lovely but his mother was glad to get him asleep."—Ralph Waldo Emerson

"Sit down and feed, and welcome to our table."—William Shakespeare

"Is it easier to be amiable, kindly, candid, with or without a headache or an attack of neuralgia?"

Chapter 3
Habit Training

Shelly had finally gotten the children in bed. With popcorn in hand and fuzzy slippers on her feet, she settled onto the couch with a sigh and pushed the Play button on the remote. She was hoping this DVD on habit training would give her a little motivation.

"The past couple of weeks we've been doing a little deep cleaning around our house," the speaker began. "Well, okay, not a little—a lot. At least it seems like a lot. Cleaning can be hard work! By the time we have the furniture moved, the closet emptied, the light fixtures disassembled, and the curtain rods dismantled, I'm tired. And only one thing keeps me going: that picture in my mind of how nice the room will look when we're done.

"We moms will work hard if we know that the goal is worth it. And what goal is more worthwhile than smooth and easy days? Isn't that what we all want in our homes?

"Charlotte Mason held that cultivating good habits in our children will bring those smooth and easy days. She said, 'We are not unwilling to make efforts in the beginning with the assurance that by-and-by things will go smoothly; and this is just what habit is, in an extraordinary degree, pledged to effect. The mother who takes pains to endow her children with good habits secures for herself smooth and easy days; while she who lets their habits take care of themselves has a weary life of endless friction with the children' (Vol. 1, p. 136)."

Shelly nodded from the couch. She could testify to that statement!

The speaker continued. "I want you to notice two important points in Charlotte's statement. First, we must 'take pains.' This habit-forming is going to require some work. But, oh, it will be worth it! Who doesn't want smooth and easy days? Smooth and easy days are worth a little effort. Smooth and easy days are worth a *lot* of effort!

"Second, the habits that we are cultivating within our children are an endowment—an investment that will bring them future benefit. Smooth and easy days now are a great goal, but this project is even bigger than that. Good habits instilled now will equip our children well for their futures.

"Think of all the habits you wish you already had ingrained in your life right now. How would they make your life easier as an adult? You have the opportunity to endow and equip your child with those habits now, and they will be in place to serve him as he grows.

"That's a goal worth hanging on the galleries of our minds. Can you picture the rewarding scenes? Then let's dedicate ourselves to working toward those smooth and easy days."

Charlotte's Thoughts on Habit Training

1. Realize that your child will not simply grow out of his faults.

"One of many ways in which parents are apt to have too low an opinion of their children is in the matter of their faults. A little child shows some ugly trait—he

---

Notes

This chapter gives some basic principles and practical tips to help you get started in this important duty of habit training. The subject of habits and habit training is examined more in-depth in Laying Down the Rails: A Charlotte Mason Habits Handbook *and the workshop by the same name, available from SimplyCharlotteMason.com.*

"The mother who takes pains to endow her children with good habits secures for herself smooth and easy days."

Notes

is greedy, and gobbles up his sister's share of the goodies as well as his own; he is vindictive, ready to bite or fight the hand that offends him; he tells a lie;—no, he did not touch the sugar-bowl or the jam-pot. The mother puts off the evil day: she knows she must sometime reckon with the child for those offences, but in the meantime she says, 'Oh, it does not matter this time; he is very little, and will know better by-and-by.' To put the thing on no higher grounds, what happy days for herself and her children would the mother secure if she would keep watch at the place of the letting out of waters! If the mother settle it in her own mind that the child never does wrong without being aware of his wrong-doing, she will see that he is not too young to have his fault corrected or prevented. Deal with a child on his *first* offence, and a grieved look is enough to convict the little transgressor; but let him go on until a habit of wrong-doing is formed, and the cure is a slow one; then the mother has no chance until she has formed in him a contrary habit of well-doing. To laugh at ugly tempers and let them pass because the child is small, is to sow the wind" (Vol. 1, p. 19).

"Here is an end to the easy philosophy of, 'It doesn't matter,' 'Oh, he'll grow out of it,' 'He'll know better by-and-by,' 'He's so young, what can we expect?' and so on. Every day, every hour, the parents are either passively or actively forming those habits in their children upon which, more than upon anything else, future character and conduct depend" (Vol. 1, p. 118).

"What you would have the man become, that you must train the child to be" (Vol. 2, p. 15).

"We found that it rests with the parents of the child to settle for the future man his ways of thinking, behaving, feeling, acting; his disposition, his particular talent; the manner of things upon which his thoughts shall run. Who shall fix limitations to the power of parents? The destiny of the child is ruled by his parents, because they have the virgin soil all to themselves. The first sowing must be at their hands, or at the hands of such as they choose to depute" (Vol. 2, p. 29).

"Get rid of the weeds and foster the flowers. It is hardly too much to say that most of the failures in life or character made by man or woman are due to the happy-go-lucky philosophy of the parents. They say, 'The child is so young; he does not know any better; but all that will come right as he grows up.' Now, a fault of character left to itself can do no other than strengthen" (Vol. 2, p. 87).

2. Your child can learn many good habits by being surrounded with them in your home.

"The whole group of habitudes, half physical and half moral, on which the propriety and comfort of everyday life depend, are received passively by the child; that is, he does very little to form these habits himself, but his brain receives impressions from what he sees about him; and these impressions take form as his own very strongest and most lasting habits.

"Cleanliness, order, neatness, regularity, punctuality, are all 'branches' of *infant* education. They should be about the child like the air he breathes, and he will take them in as unconsciously" (Vol. 1, pp. 124, 125).

> "To laugh at ugly tempers and let them pass because the child is small, is to sow the wind."

"The child's most fixed and dominant habits are those which the mother takes no pains about, but which the child picks up for himself through his close observation of all that is said and done, felt and thought, in his home.

"We have already considered a group of half-physical habits—order, regularity, neatness—which the child imbibes, so to speak, in this way. But this is not all: habits of gentleness, courtesy, kindness, candour, respect for other people, or—habits quite other than these, are inspired by the child as the very atmosphere of his home, the air he lives in and must grow by" (Vol. 1, pp. 136, 137).

"While the wide-eyed babe stretches his little person with aimless kickings on his rug, he is receiving unconsciously those first impressions which form his earliest memories; and we can order those memories for him: we can see that the earliest sights he sees are sights of order, neatness, beauty; that the sounds his ear drinks in are musical and soft, tender and joyous; that the baby's nostrils sniff only delicate purity and sweetness. These memories remain through life, engraved on the unthinking brain. As we shall see later, memories have a certain power of accretion—where there are some, others of a like kind gather, and all the life is ordered on the lines of these first pure and tender memories" (Vol. 2, pp. 26, 27).

"Thus we see how the destiny of a life is shaped in the nursery, by the reverent naming of the Divine Name; by the light scoff at holy things; by the thought of duty the little child gets who is made to finish conscientiously his little task; by the hardness of heart that comes to the child who hears the faults or sorrows of others spoken of lightly" (Vol. 2, pp. 39, 40).

3. Good habits will give you smooth and easy days now and equip your child well for the future.

"The mother who takes pains to endow her children with good habits secures for herself smooth and easy days; while she who lets their habits take care of themselves has a weary life of endless friction with the children. All day she is crying out, 'Do this!' and they do it not; 'Do that!' and they do the other" (Vol. 1, p. 136).

"The education of habit is successful in so far as it enables the mother to *let her children alone*, not teasing them with perpetual commands and directions—a running fire of *Do* and *Don't*; but letting them go their own way and *grow*, having first secured that they will go the right way, and grow to fruitful purpose. The gardener, it is true, 'digs about and dungs,' prunes and trains, his peach tree; but that occupies a small fraction of the tree's life: all the rest of the time the sweet airs and sunshine, the rains and dews, play about it and breathe upon it, get into its substance, and the result is—peaches. But let the gardener neglect *his* part, and the peaches will be no better than sloes" (Vol. 1, p. 134).

4. Determine which habits you want to instill in your child.

"Parents should take pains to have their own thoughts clear as to the manner of virtues they want their children to develop. Candour, fortitude, temperance, patience, meekness, courage, generosity, indeed the whole role of the virtues, would be stimulating subjects for thought and teaching, offering ample illustrations" (Vol. 3, p. 136).

A sloe is the small, bitter, wild fruit of the blackthorn.

"What you would have the man become, that you must train the child to be."

> "It follows that this business of laying down lines towards the unexplored country of the child's future is a very serious and responsible one for the parent. It rests with him to consider well the tracks over which the child should travel with profit and pleasure; and, along these tracks, to lay down lines so invitingly smooth and easy that the little traveller is going upon them at full speed without stopping to consider whether or no he chooses to go that way" (Vol. 1, p. 109).

5. Intentionally teach and train your child in each good character trait that you want to become a habit, using good examples, Scripture verses, and reinforcement.

> "*Kindness*, for instance, is, let us say, the subject of instruction this week. There is one of the talks with their mother that the children love—a short talk is best—about kindness. Kindness is love, showing itself in act and word, look and manner. A well of love, shut up and hidden in a little boy's heart, does not do anybody much good; the love must bubble up as a spring, flow out in a stream, and then it is *kindness*. Then will follow short daily talks about kind ways, to brothers and sisters, to playmates, to parents, to grown-up friends, to servants, to people in pain and trouble, to dumb creatures, to people we do not see but yet can think about—all in distress, the heathen. Give the children one thought at a time, and every time some lovely example of loving-kindness that will fire their hearts with the desire to do likewise.

See Romans 12:10.

> "Take our Lord's parable of the 'Good Samaritan' for a model of instruction in morals. Let tale and talk make the children emulous of virtue, and then give them the 'Go and do likewise,' the law. Having presented to them the idea of *kindness* in many aspects, end with the law: Be kind, or, 'Be kindly affectioned one to another.' Let them know that this is the law of God for children and for grown-up people. Now, conscience is instructed, the feelings are enlisted on the side of duty, and if the child is brought up, it is for breaking the law of kindness, a law that he knows of, that his conscience convicts him in the breaking" (Vol. 1, pp. 339, 340).

6. Identify any bad habit in your child and determine to set up the opposite good habit in its place.

> "A child has an odious custom, so constant, that it is his quality, will be his *character*, if you let him alone; he is spiteful, he is sly, he is sullen. No one is to blame for it; it was born in him. What are you to do with such inveterate habit of nature? Just this; treat it as a bad *habit*, and set up the opposite good habit. Henry is more than mischievous; he is a malicious little boy. There are always tears in the nursery, because, with 'pinches, nips, and bobs,' he is making some child wretched. Even his pets are not safe; he has done his canary to death by poking at it with a stick through the bars of its cage; howls from his dog, screeches from his cat, betray him in some vicious trick. He makes fearful faces at his timid little sister; sets traps with string for the housemaid with her water-cans to fall over; there is no end to the malicious tricks, beyond the mere savagery of untrained boyhood, which come to his mother's ear. What is to be done? 'Oh, he will grow out of it!' say the more hopeful who pin their faith to time. But many an experienced mother will say, 'You can't cure him; what is in will out, and he will be a pest to society all his life.' Yet the child may be cured in a month if the mother will set herself to the task with both

"Treat it as a bad habit, and set up the opposite good habit."

7. See that your child does the new good habit as much as possible for at least a month.

"Let the month of treatment be a deliciously happy month to him, he living all the time in the sunshine of his mother's smile. Let him not be left to himself to meditate or carry out ugly pranks. Let him feel himself always under a watchful, loving, and *approving* eye. Keep him happily occupied, well amused. All this, to break the old custom which is assuredly broken when a certain length of time goes by without its repetition. But one habit drives out another. Lay new lines in the old place. Open avenues of kindness for him. Let him enjoy, daily, hourly, the pleasure of pleasing. Get him into the way of making little plots for the pleasure of the rest—a plaything of his contriving, a dish of strawberries of his gathering, shadow rabbits to amuse the baby; take him on kind errands to poor neighbours, carrying and giving of his own. For a whole month the child's whole heart is flowing out in deeds and schemes and thoughts of lovingkindness, and the ingenuity which spent itself in malicious tricks becomes an acquisition to his family when his devices are benevolent" (Vol. 2, pp. 86, 87).

8. Devote yourself to the correction of a bad habit as you would to nursing a sick child.

"Yes; but where is his mother to get time in these encroaching days to put Henry under special treatment? She has other children and other duties, and simply cannot give herself up for a month or a week to one child. If the boy were ill, in danger, would she find time for him then? Would not other duties go to the wall, and leave her little son, for the time, her chief object in life?

"Now here is a point all parents are not enough awake to—that serious mental and moral ailments require prompt, purposeful, curative treatment, to which the parents must devote themselves for a short time, just as they would to a sick child" (Vol. 2, p. 87).

9. Keep a diary to help you oversee your child's progress in character and good habits.

"Every mother, especially, should keep a diary in which to note the successive phases of her child's physical, mental, and moral growth, with particular attention to the moral; so that parents may be enabled to make a timely forecast of their children's character, to foster in them every germ of good, and by prompt precautions to suppress, or at least restrain, what is bad" (Vol. 2, pp. 105, 106).

10. Depend on the Lord's help and pray for your child during habit training.

"Here, indeed, more than anywhere, 'Except the Lord build the house, they labour but in vain that build it'; but surely intelligent co-operation in this divine work is our bounden duty and service. The training of the will, the instruction of the conscience, and, so far as it lies with us, the development of the divine life in the child, are carried on simultaneously with this training in the habits of a good life; and these last will carry the child safely over the season of infirm will, immature conscience, until he is able to take, under direction from above, the conduct of his

---

Notes

A handy checklist is included in Laying Down the Rails, *along with practical tips for the sixty habits Charlotte recommended we cultivate in our children.*

"It is well to clear our thoughts and know definitely what we desire for our children."

Notes

Mauvaise honte *is a false sense of embarrassment.*

Character is the result of habits. A person who is known for being truthful, for example, habitually tells the truth; he doesn't tell the truth only once in a while. Telling the truth is a habit ingrained in his life.

"The child of two should be taught to get and to replace his playthings."

---

life, the moulding of his character, into his own hands" (Vol. 2, p. 90).

"This kind cometh forth only by prayer, but it is well to clear our thoughts and know definitely what we desire for our children, because only so can we work intelligently towards the fulfilment of our desire. It is sad to pray, and frustrate the answer by our own action; but this is, alas, too possible" (Vol. 2, p. 289).

11. One good habit you might want to instill would be to teach your two-year-old to put away his toys.

"The child of two should be taught to get and to replace his playthings. Begin early. Let it be a pleasure to him, part of his play, to open his cupboard, and put back the doll or the horse each in its own place. Let him *always* put away his things as a matter of course, and it is surprising how soon a habit of order is formed, which will make it pleasant to the child to put away his toys, and irritating to him to see things in the wrong place. If parents would only see the morality of order, that order in the nursery becomes scrupulousness in after life, and that the training necessary to form the habit is no more, comparatively, than the occasional winding of a clock, which ticks away then of its own accord and without trouble to itself, more pains would be taken to cultivate this important habit" (Vol. 1, p. 130).

12. You can also practice good manners by role-playing with your child.

"Just let them go through the drill of good manners: let them rehearse little scenes in play—Mary, the lady asking the way to the market; Harry, the boy who directs her, and so on. Let them go through a position drill—eyes right, hands still, heads up. They will invent a hundred situations, and the behaviour proper to each, and will treasure hints thrown in for their guidance; but this sort of drill should be attempted while children are young, before the tyranny of *mauvaise honte* sets in" (Vol. 1, pp. 132, 133).

13. Train your child to be habitually truthful.

"The child who appears to be perfectly truthful is so because he has been carefully trained to truthfulness, however indirectly and unconsciously. It is more important to cultivate the habit of truth than to deal with the accident of lying" (Vol. 2, p. 213).

14. Teach your child to unselfishly give, share, and serve. This habit will deter a mind-set of "It's not fair" later in life.

"A child who is taught from the first the delights of giving and sharing, of loving and bearing, will always spend himself freely on others, will love and serve, seeking for nothing again; but the child who recognises that he is the object of constant attention, consideration, love and service, becomes self-regardful, self-seeking, selfish, almost without his fault, so strongly is he influenced by the direction his thoughts receive from those about him. So, too, of that other fountain, of justice, with which every child is born. There, again, the stream may flow forth in either, but not in both, of the channels, the egoistic or the altruistic. The child's demand for justice may be all for himself, or, from the very first, the rights of others may be kept before his eyes.

"He may be taught to occupy himself with *his own rights and other people's duties*, and, if he is, his state of mind is easily discernible by the catchwords often on his lips, 'It's a shame!' 'It's not fair!' or he may, on the other hand, be so filled with the notion of *his own duties and other people's rights*, that the claims of self slip quietly into the background" (Vol. 2, pp. 288, 289).

Questions to Ask about Habit Training

- Do I fully realize that my child will not just grow out of his faults?
- Do I believe that my child can learn many good habits by being surrounded with them in my home?
- Have I caught the vision that habit training now will provide smooth and easy days plus equip my child well for the future?
- Have I determined which habits I want to instill in my child?
- Am I intentionally teaching and training my child in each good character trait that I want to become a habit, using good examples, Scripture verses, and reinforcement?
- Am I carefully identifying any bad habit in my child and working to set up the opposite good habit in its place?
- Am I trying to see that my child does the new good habit as much as possible for at least a month?
- Am I willing to devote myself to the correction of a bad habit as I would to nursing a sick child?
- Do I keep a diary to help me oversee my child's progress in character and good habits?
- Am I depending on the Lord's help and praying for my child during habit training?
- Am I trying to teach my two-year-old to put away his toys?
- Am I training my child in good manners by practicing and role-playing?
- Am I seeking to train my child to be habitually truthful?
- Am I teaching my child to unselfishly give, share, and serve?

More Quotes on Habit Training

"It is easier to build strong children than to repair broken men."—Frederick Douglass

"A nail is driven out by another nail, habit is overcome by habit."—Desiderius Gerhard Erasmus

"Cultivate only the habits that you are willing should master you."—Elbert Hubbard

"The child is father of the man."—William Wordsworth

"The child who appears to be perfectly truthful is so because he has been carefully trained to truthfulness."

Notes

Of all Charlotte's writings on habits, she wrote the most about Attention, Obedience, and Truthfulness.

"First, we put the habit of Attention."

The Habit of Attention

(Charlotte wrote a conversation between a mother and the long-time family doctor that presents some key elements of training a child in the habit of attention. Here is the conversation, taken from Volume 5, pages 94 and 95.)

"Pray, ma'am, what would you like me to say next?"

"To 'habit,' doctor, to 'habit'; and don't talk nonsense while the precious time is going. We'll suppose that Fred is just twelve months old to-day. Now, if you please, tell me how I'm to make him *begin* to pay attention. And, by the way, why in the world didn't you talk to me about it when the child really was young?"

"I don't remember that you asked me; and who would be pert enough to think of schooling a young mother? Not I, at any rate. Don't I know that every mother of a first child is infallible, and knows more about children than all the old doctors in creation? But, supposing you had asked me, I should have said—Get him each day to occupy himself a little longer with one plaything than he did the day before. He plucks a daisy, gurgles over it with glee, and then in an instant it drops from the nerveless grasp. Then you take it up, and with the sweet coaxings you mothers know how to employ, get him to examine it, in his infant fashion, for a minute, two minutes, three whole minutes at a time."

"I see; fix his thoughts on one thing at a time, and for as long as you can, whether on what he sees or what he hears. You think if you go on with that sort of thing with a child from his infancy he gets accustomed to pay attention?"

"Not a doubt of it; and you may rely on it that what is called *ability*—a different thing from genius, mind you, or even talent—ability is simply the power of fixing the attention steadily on the matter in hand, and success in life turns upon this cultivated power far more than on any natural faculty. Lay a case before a successful barrister, an able man of business, notice how he absorbs all you say; tell your tale as ill as you like, he keeps the thread, straightens the tangle, and by the time you have finished, has the whole matter spread out in order under his mind's eye. Now comes in talent, or genius, or what you will, to deal with the facts he has taken in. But attention is the attribute of the trained intellect, without which genius makes shots in the dark."

"But, don't you think attention itself is a natural faculty, or talent, or whatever we should call it?"

"Not a bit of it; it is entirely the result of training. A man may be born with some faculty or talent for figures, or drawing, or music, but attention is a different matter; it is simply the power of bending such powers as one has to the work in hand; it is a key to success within the reach of every one, but the skill to turn it comes of training. Circumstances may compel a man to train himself, but he does so at the cost of great effort, and the chances are ten to one against his making the effort. For the child, on the other hand, who has been trained by his parents to fix his thoughts, all is plain sailing. He will succeed, not a doubt of it."

Charlotte's Thoughts on the Habit of Attention

1. The habit of attention should be a top priority.

"First, we put the *habit of Attention*, because the highest intellectual gifts depend for their value upon the measure in which their owner has cultivated the habit of attention" (Vol. 1, p. 137).

"Whatever the natural gifts of the child, it is only so far as the habit of attention is cultivated in him that he is able to make use of them" (Vol. 1, p. 146).

2. Recognize that it is hard for a young child to force himself to stop making mental associations, which is what leads to inattention.

"You talk to a child about glass—you wish to provoke a proper curiousity as to how glass is made, and what are its uses. Not a bit of it; he wanders off to Cinderella's glass slipper; then he tells you about *his* godmother who gave him a boat; then about the ship in which Uncle Harry went to America; then he wonders why you do not wear spectacles, leaving you to guess that Uncle Harry does so. But the child's ramblings are not whimsical; they follow a law, the law of association of ideas, by which any idea presented to the mind recalls some other idea which has been at any time associated with it—as glass, and Cinderella's slipper; and that, again some idea associated with it. Now this law of association of ideas is a good servant and a bad master. To have this aid in recalling the events of the past, the engagements of the present, is an infinite boon; but to be at the mercy of associations, to have no power to think of what we choose when we choose, but only as something 'puts it in our head,' is to be no better than an imbecile.

"A vigorous effort of will should enable us at any time to fix our thoughts. Yes; but a vigorous self-compelling will is the flower of a developed character; and while the child has no character to speak of, but only natural disposition, who is to keep humming-tops out of a geography lesson, or a doll's sofa out of a French verb?" (Vol. 1, pp. 138, 139).

3. Encourage your infant or young child to strengthen and expand his attention span little by little.

"The help, then, is not the will of the child but in the *habit of attention*, a habit to be cultivated even in the infant. A baby, notwithstanding his wonderful powers of observation, has no power of attention; in a minute, the coveted plaything drops from listless little fingers, and the wandering glance lights upon some new joy. But even at this stage the habit of attention may be trained: the discarded plaything is picked up, and, with 'Pretty!' and dumb [silent] show, the mother keeps the infant's eyes fixed for fully a couple of minutes—and this is his first lesson in attention. Later, as we have seen, the child is eager to see and handle every object that comes in his way. But watch him at his investigations: he flits from thing to thing with less purpose than a butterfly amongst the flowers, staying at nothing long enough to get the good out of it. It is the mother's part to supplement the child's quick observing faculty with the habit of attention. She must see to it that he does not flit from this to that, but looks long enough at one thing to get a real acquaintance with it.

"Is little Margaret fixing round eyes on a daisy she has plucked? In a second, the daisy will be thrown away, and a pebble or a buttercup will charm the little maid. But the mother seizes the happy moment. She makes Margaret see that the daisy is a bright yellow eye with *white* eyelashes round it; that all the day long it lies there in the grass and looks up at the great sun, never blinking as Margaret would do, but keeping its eyes wide open. And that is why it is called daisy, 'day's eye,' because

> "The mother will contrive ways to invest every object in the child's world with interest and delight."

Habit Training

Notes

For more on the habit of attention, see Laying Down the Rails: A Charlotte Mason Habits Handbook.

its eye is always looking at the sun which makes the day. And what does Margaret think it does at night, when there is no sun? It does what little boys and girls do; it just shuts up its eye with its white lashes tipped with pink, and goes to sleep till the sun comes again in the morning. By this time the daisy has become interesting to Margaret; she looks at it with big eyes after her mother has finished speaking, and then, very likely, cuddles it up to her breast or gives it a soft little kiss. Thus the mother will contrive ways to invest every object in the child's world with interest and delight" (Vol. 1, pp. 139, 140).

4. Laying a foundation of the habit of attention during the early years will make the school years much smoother.

"Attention is the power and habit of concentrating every faculty on the thing in hand. Now this habit of attention, parents, mothers especially, are taught to encourage and cultivate in their children from early infancy. What you regard with full attention, if only for a minute, you know, and remember always. Think of the few scenes and conversations we, each, have so vividly fixed that we cannot possibly forget them. Why? Because at the moment our attention was powerfully excited. You reap some benefit from this early training directly the boy goes to school" (Vol. 5, pp. 164, 165).

Questions to Ask about the Habit of Attention

- Am I doing what I can to make the habit of attention top priority?
- Do I recognize that it's hard for my child to control mental associations that lead to inattention?
- Am I encouraging my infant or young child to strengthen and expand his attention span little by little?
- Do I realize that instilling the habit of attention now will make future school years much smoother?

More Quotes on the Habit of Attention

"The true art of memory is the art of attention."—Samuel Johnson

"If I have ever made any valuable discoveries, it has been owing more to patient attention, than to any other talent."—Isaac Newton

"What you regard with full attention, if only for a minute, you know, and remember always."

The Habit of Obedience

"What am I doing wrong, Mom?" wailed Evette into the telephone. "Every time I'm on the phone, Joey thinks he can get away with anything. He doesn't obey me until I've repeated myself at least ten times and raised my voice. I don't know what to do!"

"Well, first, dear," replied Mrs. Common, "stop whining and lower your voice. I'm sure Joey can hear what you're saying."

"He's outside in the sandbox, Mom," Evette explained. "It's okay." But she did take a deep breath and tried to relax her shoulders.

Mrs. Common continued, "I have three pieces of advice for you. Number One, stay off the phone until you have developed in Joey the habit of prompt obedience. Let the answering machine do its job."

"But Mom," Evette objected, "the phone is how I stay connected to my friends. I love to chat with Susie and Rachel."

"I know, honey, but you have a crisis on your hands right now," Mrs. Common said. "If you want things to change, you will need to give this your undivided attention. And that includes time on the Internet too."

"This is going to be hard, but I've got to do something," agreed Evette.

"Number Two, decide right now who is going to be in charge at your house."

"Some days it feels like Joey is running the show, I'll admit."

"Then you need to settle it in your mind that God has placed you in authority, Evette," said Mrs. Common. "That mind-set can make all the difference, and it will show in the way you interact with Joey. You should expect prompt obedience. There is no need to bribe, threaten, or yell."

"But what do I do when he doesn't obey until the tenth time I say something?" Evette asked.

"Let me ask you this: Why does he obey that tenth time?"

"Because he knows he will receive a consequence if he doesn't," replied Evette.

"Exactly. So Number Three, apply the consequence sooner. If you want Joey to obey after you raise your voice, then wait and apply the consequence after you raise your voice," explained Mrs. Common. "If you want Joey to obey after a single telling, then apply the consequence after that single telling."

"Makes sense," said Evette.

"But it will work only if you give it your full attention for at least a month," Mrs. Common cautioned. "By then, if you are consistent, Joey will have developed the habit of prompt obedience, and your days will be much smoother and easier."

"Okay, Mom, I'll give it a try," Evette said. "Thanks for your help."

"You're welcome," Mrs. Common replied. "And Evette?"

"Yes?"

"You're a good mommy."

Charlotte's Thoughts on the Habit of Obedience

1. Realize that obedience is the whole duty of the child and is for his good.

"First, and infinitely the most important, is the habit of *obedience*. Indeed, obedience is the whole duty of the child, and for this reason—every other duty of the child is fulfilled as a matter of obedience to his parents. Not only so: obedience is the whole duty of man; obedience to conscience, to law, to Divine direction" (Vol. 1, p. 161).

"What is the object of family discipline, of that obedience which has been described as 'the whole duty of a child'? Is it not to ease the way of the child, while will is weak and conscience immature, by getting it on the habits of the good life where it is as easy to go right as for a locomotive to run on its lines?" (Vol. 2, p. 166).

"If we wish children to be able, when they grow up, to keep under their bodies and bring them into subjection, we must do this *for* them in their earlier years."

Notes

For Charlotte's thoughts on parental authority, see Volume 2, pages 10–18.

"If we wish children to be able, when they grow up, to keep under their bodies and bring them into subjection, we must do this *for* them in their earlier years" (Vol. 3, p. 19).

"It is an old story that the failures in life are not the people who lack good intentions; they are those whose physical nature has not acquired the habit of prompt and involuntary obedience. The man who can make himself do what he wills has the world before him, and it rests with parents to give their children this self-compelling power as a mere matter of habit" (Vol. 3, p. 20).

2. Teach your young child the meaning of must.

"Who has not met big girls and boys, the children of right-minded parents, who yet do not know what *must* means, who are not moved by *ought*, whose hearts feel no stir at the solemn name of *Duty*, who know no higher rule of life than 'I want,' and 'I don't want,' 'I like,' and 'I don't like'? Heaven help parents and children when it has come to that!" (Vol. 1, p. 14).

" 'I teach my children obedience by the time they are one year old,' the writer heard a very successful mother remark; and, indeed, that is the age at which to begin to give children the ease and comfort of the habit of obeying lawful authority" (Vol. 3, p. 18).

3. Be careful of teaching your child that obedience doesn't matter by laughing at his disobedience.

"But how has it been brought about that the babe, with an acute sense of right and wrong even when it can understand little of human speech, should grow into the boy or girl already proving 'the curse of lawless heart'? By slow degrees, here a little and there a little, as all that is good or bad in character comes to pass. 'Naughty!' says the mother, again, when a little hand is thrust into the sugar-bowl; and a pair of roguish eyes seeks hers furtively, to measure, as they do unerringly, how far the little pilferer may go. It is very amusing; the mother 'cannot help laughing'; and the little trespass is allowed to pass: and, what the poor mother has not thought of, an offence, a cause of stumbling, has been cast into the path of her two-year-old child. He has learned already that that which is 'naughty' may yet be done with impunity, and he goes on improving his knowledge" (Vol. 1, pp. 14, 15).

4. Be pleasantly consistent. Once a child discovers that mother is inconsistent, he steps down the path to disobedience.

"She *must not* let him break his sister's playthings, gorge himself with cake, spoil the pleasure of other people, because these things are not right."

"It is needless to continue; everybody knows the steps by which the mother's 'no' comes to be disregarded, her refusal teased into consent. The child has learned to believe that he has nothing to overcome but his mother's disinclination; if she *choose* to let him do this and that, there is no reason why she should not; he can make her choose to let him do the thing forbidden, and then he may do it. The next step in the argument is not too great for childish wits: if his mother does what she chooses, of course he will do what he chooses, *if he can;* and henceforward the child's life becomes an endless struggle to get his own way; a struggle in which a parent is pretty sure to be worsted, having many things to think of, while the child sticks persistently to the thing which has his fancy for the moment" (Vol. 1, p. 15).

5. Remember that you are on assignment from God to teach your child to do right.

"Where is the beginning of this tangle, spoiling the lives of parent and child alike? In this: that the mother began with no sufficient sense of duty; she thought herself free to allow and disallow, to say and unsay, at pleasure, as if the child were hers to do what she liked with. The child has never discovered a background of *must* behind his mother's decisions; he does not know that she *must not* let him break his sister's playthings, gorge himself with cake, spoil the pleasure of other people, because these things are not *right*. Let the child perceive that his parents are law-compelled as well as he, that they simply cannot allow him to do the things which have been forbidden, and he submits with the sweet meekness which belongs to his age" (Vol. 1, p. 15).

"It is well that a child should be taught to keep under his body and bring it into subjection, first, to the authority of his parents and, later, to the authority of his own will; and always, because no less than this is due, to the divine Authority in whom he has his being" (Vol. 3, p. 104).

"Now, if the parent realise that obedience is no mere accidental duty, the fulfilling of which is a matter that lies between himself and the child, but that he is the appointed agent to train the child up to the intelligent obedience of the self-compelling, law-abiding human being, he will see that he has no right to *forego* the obedience of his child, and that every act of disobedience in the child is a direct condemnation of the parent. Also, he will see that the motive of the child's obedience is not the arbitrary one of, 'Do this, or that, because I have said so,' but the motive of the apostolic injunction, 'Children, obey your parents in the Lord, *for this is right*' " (Vol. 1, p. 161).

6. Understand that training in obedience "for this is right" and bullying a child to do what you want are two completely different things.

"It is only in proportion as the will of the child is in the act of obedience, and he obeys because his sense of *right* makes him *desire* to obey in spite of temptations to disobedience—not of constraint, but willingly—that the habit has been formed which will, hereafter, enable the child to use the strength of his will against his inclinations when these prompt him to lawless courses. It is said that the children of parents who are most strict in exacting obedience often turn out ill; and that orphans and other poor waifs brought up under strict discipline only wait their opportunity to break out into license. Exactly so; because, in these cases, there is no gradual training of the child in the *habit* of obedience; no gradual enlisting of his *will* on the side of sweet service and a free-will offering of submission to the highest law: the poor children are simply bullied into submission to the *will*, that is, the *wilfulness*, of another; not at all, 'for it is *right*'; only because it is convenient" (Vol. 1, pp. 161, 162).

7. Expect obedience and communicate that expectation in your voice and demeanor.

"The mother has no more sacred duty than that of training her infant to instant obedience. . . . There is no need to rate the child, or threaten him, or use any

> "The mother has no more sacred duty than that of training her infant to instant obedience."

manner of violence, because the parent is *invested* with authority which the child intuitively recognises. It is enough to say, 'Do this,' in a quiet, authoritative tone, and *expect it to be done*. The mother often enough loses her hold over her children because they detect in the tone of her voice that she does not expect them to obey her behests; she does not think enough of her position; has not sufficient confidence in her own authority. The mother's great stronghold is in the *habit* of obedience. If she begin by requiring that her children always obey her, why, they will always do so as a matter of course; but let them once get the thin end of the wedge in, let them discover that they can do otherwise than obey, and a woful struggle begins, which commonly ends in the children doing that which is right in their own eyes" (Vol. 1, pp. 162, 163).

8. Reasoning with a young child is usually futile and unnecessary.

"To give reasons to a child is usually out of place, and is a sacrifice of parental dignity; but he is quick enough to read the 'must' and 'ought' which rule her, in his mother's face and manner, and in the fact that she is not to be moved from a resolution on any question of right and wrong" (Vol. 1, pp. 15, 16).

9. Insist from the first on prompt, cheerful, lasting obedience every time.

"This is the sort of thing which is fatal: The children are in the drawing-room, and a caller is announced. 'You must go upstairs now.' 'Oh, mother dear, *do* let us stay in the window-corner; we will be as quiet as mice!' The mother is rather proud of her children's pretty manners, and they stay. They are *not* quiet, of course; but that is the least of the evils; they have succeeded in doing as they chose and not as they were bid, and they will not put their necks under the yoke again without a struggle. It is in little matters that the mother is worsted. 'Bedtime, Willie!' 'Oh, mamma, *just* let me finish this'; and the mother yields, forgetting that the case in point is of no consequence; the thing that matters is that the child should be daily confirming a *habit* of obedience by the unbroken repetition of acts of obedience. It is astonishing how clever the child is in finding ways of evading the spirit while he observes the letter. 'Mary, come in.' 'Yes, mother'; but her mother calls four times before Mary comes. 'Put away your bricks'; and the bricks are put away with slow, reluctant fingers. 'You must *always* wash your hands when you hear the first bell.' The child obeys for that once, and no more.

"To avoid these displays of wilfulness, the mother will insist from the first on an obedience which is prompt, cheerful, and lasting—save for lapses of memory on the child's part. Tardy, unwilling, occasional obedience is hardly worth the having; and it is greatly easier to give the child the *habit* of perfect obedience by never allowing him in anything else, than it is to obtain this mere formal obedience by a constant exercise of authority" (Vol. 1, pp. 163, 164).

10. When the child is old enough, discuss the noble effort of making yourself obey.

"By-and-by, when he is old enough, take the child into confidence; let him know what a noble thing it is to be able to make himself do, in a minute, and brightly, the very thing he would rather not do" (Vol. 1, p. 164).

> "To give reasons to a child is usually out of place."

11. Never give a command that you do not intend to see fully carried out.

"To secure this habit of obedience, the mother must exercise great self-restraint; she must never give a command which she does not intend to see carried out to the full" (Vol. 1, p. 164).

12. Don't pester your child with incessant commands.

"And she must not lay upon her children burdens, grievous to be borne, of command heaped upon command" (Vol. 1, p. 164).

13. Take courage from the fact that once the habit of obedience is instilled, you and your child will enjoy a great deal of liberty.

"The children who are trained to perfect obedience may be trusted with a good deal of liberty: they receive a few directions which they know they must not disobey; and for the rest, they are left to learn how to direct their own actions, even at the cost of some small mishaps; and are not pestered with a perpetual fire of 'Do this,' and 'Don't do that!'" (Vol. 1, p. 164).

Questions to Ask about the Habit of Obedience

- Do I believe that obedience is my child's duty and is for his good?
- Am I working hard to teach my child the meaning of *must*?
- Am I being careful not to laugh at my child's disobedience?
- Am I trying to be pleasantly consistent?
- Do I understand that I am on assignment from God to teach my child to do right?
- Am I being careful to train my child in obedience but not bully him?
- Am I expecting my child to obey and communicating that expectation in my voice and demeanor?
- Am I comfortable in my position as the God-appointed authority, or do I feel the need to try to reason with my child?
- Am I trying to insist on prompt, cheerful, lasting obedience every time?
- Have I discussed with my older child the noble effort it takes to obey?
- Am I being careful never to give a command that I do not intend to see fully carried out?
- Am I trying not to pester my child with incessant commands?
- Am I keeping the future goal of liberty in mind as I train my child in the habit of obedience?

More Quotes on the Habit of Obedience

"Let the child's first lesson be obedience, and the second will be what thou wilt."—Benjamin Franklin

"Children, obey your parents in the Lord: for this is right."—Ephesians 6:1

Notes

For more on the habit of obedience, see Laying Down the Rails: A Charlotte Mason Habits Handbook.

"She must never give a command which she does not intend to see carried out to the full."

Part 3

Nourish the Mind on Loving, Right, and Noble Ideas

Chapter 4
Using the Senses

Brady was helping Mommy set the table.

"Be sure Daddy gets a big fork, honey," said Mom.

Brady looked up from his job, uncertain.

Mommy picked two forks out of the silverware stacked on the table. She held up a big fork and a smaller fork, resting the ends of their handles on the table, so Brady could see them beside each other.

"See?" she explained. "One of these forks is bigger . . . " she wiggled the big fork, "and one is smaller. Let's see if you can put the big fork at Dad's place."

She handed both forks to Brady with a smile. Brady held them up just like she had done, then placed the big fork beside Dad's plate.

"Good job, sweetie," Mom said. She handed him another big fork. "Mom gets a big fork too."

Once again Brady compared the two forks and placed the big one correctly.

"That's right," said Mom. "And the smaller fork goes at your place."

Charlotte's Thoughts on Using the Senses

1. A young child uses his five senses to learn about everything around him.

"In his early years the child is all eyes; he observes, or, more truly, he perceives, calling sight, touch, taste, smell, and hearing to his aid, that he may learn all that is discoverable by him about every new thing that comes under his notice. Everybody knows how a baby fumbles over with soft little fingers, and carries to his mouth, and bangs that it may produce what sound there is in it, the spoon or doll which supercilious grown-up people give him to 'keep him quiet.' The child is at his lessons, and is learning all about it at a rate utterly surprising to the physiologist, who considers how much is implied in the act of 'seeing,' for instance: that to the infant, as to the blind adult restored to sight, there is at first no difference between a flat picture and a solid body,—that the ideas of form and solidity are not obtained by sight at all, but are the judgments of experience" (Vol. 1, p. 65).

"My object is to show that the chief function of the child—his business in the world during the first six or seven years of his life—is to find out all he can, about whatever comes under his notice, by means of his five senses; that he has an insatiable appetite for knowledge got in this way; and that, therefore, the endeavour of his parents should be to put him in the way of making acquaintance freely with Nature and natural objects" (Vol. 1, p. 96).

"That the knowledge most valuable to the child is that which he gets with his own eyes and ears and fingers (under direction) in the open air" (Vol. 1, p. 177).

"His progress is amazing. At first he does not see any difference between a picture of a cow and the living animal; big and little, far and near, hard and soft,

> "The chief function of the child—his business in the world during the first six or seven years of his life—is to find out all he can, about whatever comes under his notice, by means of his five senses."

hot and cold, are all alike to him; he wishes to hold the moon in his pinafore, to sit on the pond, to poke his finger into the candle, not because he is a foolish little person, but because he is profoundly ignorant of the nature of the contents of this unintelligible world. But how he works! he bangs his spoon to try if it produces sound; he sucks it to try its flavour; he fumbles it all over and no doubt finds out whether it is hard or soft, hot or cold, rough or smooth; he gazes at it with the long gaze of infancy, so that he may learn the look of it; it is an old friend and an object of desire when he sees it again, for he has found out that there is much joy in a spoon. This goes on with great diligence for a couple of years, at the end of which time baby has acquired enough knowledge of the world to conduct himself in a very dignified and rational way" (Vol. 2, p. 181).

2. A young child will proceed with his learning at the right pace for him.

"Then, think of the vague passes in the air the little fist makes before it lays hold of the object of desire, and you see how he learns the whereabouts of things, having as yet no idea of direction. And why does he cry for the moon? Why does he crave equally, a horse or a house-fly as an appropriate plaything? Because far and near, large and small, are ideas he has yet to grasp. The child has truly a great deal to do before he is in a condition to 'believe his own eyes'; but Nature teaches so gently, so gradually, so persistently, that he is never overdone, but goes on gathering little stores of knowledge about whatever comes before him" (Vol. 1, p. 66).

3. This learning through the senses is important because it lays the foundation for future understanding.

"And this is the process the child should continue for the first few years of his life. Now is the storing time which should be spent in laying up images of things familiar. By-and-by he will have to *conceive* of things he has never seen: how can he do it except by comparison with things he has seen and knows? By-and-by he will be called upon to reflect, understand, reason; what material will he have, unless he has a magazine of facts to go upon? The child who has been made to observe how high in the heavens the sun is at noon on a summer's day, how low at noon on a day in mid-winter, is able to *conceive* of the great heat of the tropics under a vertical sun, and to *understand* that the climate of a place depends greatly upon the mean height the sun reaches above the horizon" (Vol. 1, p. 66).

"There is no end to the store of common information, got in such a way that it will never be forgotten, with which an intelligent child may furnish himself before he begins his school career" (Vol. 1, p. 68).

"The intellectual education of the young child should lie in the free exercise of perceptive power, because the first stages of mental effort are marked by the extreme activity of this power" (Vol. 1, pp. 96, 97).

"Equally strong, equally natural, equally sure of awakening a responsive stir in the young soul, is the divinely implanted principle of curiosity. The child *wants to know*; wants to know incessantly, desperately; asks all manner of questions about everything he comes across, plagues his elders and betters, and is told not to bother, and to be a good boy and not ask questions. But this only sometimes. For the most part we lay ourselves out to answer Tommy's questions so far as we are able, and are sadly ashamed that we are so soon floored by his insatiable curiosity about natural objects and phenomena" (Vol. 2, p. 221).

"The most surprising educational feat accomplished amongst us is the amount of knowledge, about everything within his range, which Tommy has acquired by the end of his sixth year. 'Why, he knows as much as I do, about'—this, and that, and the other, says his astonished and admiring father. Take him to the seaside, and in a week he will tell you all about trawling and mackerel fishing, the ways of the fisherfolk, and all that his inquisitive mind can find out unaided. He would tell all about sand, and shells, and tides, and waves, only, poor little boy, he must have help towards this manner of knowledge, and there is no one to give it to him. However, he finds out all that he can about all that he sees and hears, and does amass a surprising amount of exact knowledge about things and their properties" (Vol. 2, p. 221).

4. A young child can do a great amount of mental work without stress if it is the right kind of work: using his senses to examine new objects.

"A great deal has been said lately about the danger of overpressure, of requiring too much mental work from a child of tender years. The danger exists; but lies, not in giving the child too much, but in giving him the wrong thing to do, the sort of work for which the present state of his mental development does not fit him. Who expects a boy in petticoats to lift half a hundredweight? But give the child work that Nature intended for him, and the quantity he can get through with ease is practically unlimited. Whoever saw a child tired of seeing, of examining in his own way, unfamiliar things? This is the sort of mental nourishment for which he has an unbounded appetite, because it is that food of the mind on which, for the present, he is meant to grow" (Vol. 1, pp. 66, 67).

"For the first five or six years of his life, everything, especially everything in action, is an object of intelligent curiosity to the child—the street or the field is a panorama of delight, the shepherd's dog, the baker's cart, the man with the barrow, are full of vivid interest. He has a thousand questions to ask, he wants to know about everything; he has, in fact, an inordinate appetite for knowledge. We soon cure all that: we occupy him with books instead of things; we evoke other desires in place of the desire to know; and we succeed in bringing up the unobservant man (and more unobservant woman) who discerns no difference between an elm, a poplar and a lime tree, and misses very much of the joy of living" (Vol. 2, pp. 181, 182).

5. An observant child should be put in the way of things worth observing.

"Now, consider what a culpable waste of intellectual energy it is to shut up a child, blessed with this inordinate capacity for seeing and knowing, within the four walls of a house, or the dreary streets of a town. Or suppose that he is let run loose in the country where there is plenty to see, it is nearly as bad to let this great faculty of the child's dissipate itself in random observations for want of method and direction" (Vol. 1, p. 68).

> "Now, consider what a culpable waste of intellectual energy it is to shut up a child, blessed with this inordinate capacity for seeing and knowing, within the four walls of a house."

Using the Senses

Notes

Object lessons are bringing various items from nature into the room and letting the child examine them as you tell about them.

In situ means "in the place" and refers to natural habitat or environment.

"Object-lessons should be incidental; and this is where the family enjoys so great an advantage over the school."

"But what is the use of being a 'very observant child,' if you are not put in the way of things worth observing? And here is the difference between the streets of a town and the sights and sounds of the country. There is plenty to be seen in a town, and children accustomed to the ways of the streets become nimble-witted enough. But the scraps of information to be picked up in a town are isolated fragments; they do not hang on to anything else, nor come to anything more; the information may be convenient, but no one is the wiser for knowing which side of the street is Smith's, and which turning leads to Thompson's shop" (Vol. 1, pp. 69, 70).

"Two points call for our attention in the education of the senses; we must assist the child to educate himself on Nature's lines, and we must take care not to supplant and crowd out Nature and her methods with that which we call education" (Vol. 2, p. 182).

6. Formal object lessons provide some opportunity for a young child to use his senses to learn, but they do not "spread a feast" for him.

"Now, how far is this craving for natural sustenance met? In infant and kindergarten schools, by the object lesson, which is good so far as it goes, but is sometimes like that bean a day on which the Frenchman fed his horse. The child at home has more new things brought under his notice, if with less method. Neither at home nor at school is much effort made to set before the child the abundant 'feast of eyes' which his needs demand" (Vol. 1, p. 67).

"The purpose of so-called object-lessons is to assist a child, by careful examination of a given object, to find out all he can about it through the use of his several senses. General information about the object is thrown in, and lodges only because the child's senses have been exercised and his interest aroused. Object-lessons are a little in disfavour just now, for two reasons. In the first place, miserable fragments are presented to the children which have little of the character of the object *in situ*, and are apt to convey inadequate, if not wrong, ideas. In the next place, object-lessons are commonly used as a means to introduce children to hard words, such as opaque and translucent, which never become part of their living thought until they pick them up for themselves incidentally as they have need of them. But the abuse of this kind of teaching should not cause us to overlook its use. No child can grow up without daily object teaching, whether casual or of set purpose; and the more thorough this is, the more intelligent and observant will he become. It is singular how few people are capable of developing an intelligent curiosity about the most attractive objects, except as their interest is stimulated from without" (Vol. 2, pp. 180, 181).

7. Family life offers an advantage in everyday, on-the-spot, natural object lessons.

"Object-lessons should be incidental; and this is where the family enjoys so great an advantage over the school. It is almost impossible that the school should give any but set lessons; but this sort of teaching in the family falls in with the occurrence of the object. The child who finds that wonderful and beautiful object, a 'paper' wasp's nest, attached to a larch-twig, has his object-lesson on the spot from father or mother. The grey colour, the round symmetrical shape, the sort of cup-

and-ball arrangement, the papery texture, the comparative size, the comparative smoothness, the odour or lack of odour, the extreme lightness, the fact that it is not cold to the touch—these and fifty other particulars the child finds out unaided, or with no more than a word, here and there, to direct his observation. One does not find a wasp's nest every day, but much can be got out of every common object, and the commoner the better, which falls naturally under the child's observation, a piece of bread, a lump of coal, a sponge" (Vol. 2, pp. 182, 183).

"We should fill for children the storehouse of memory with many open-air images, capable of giving them reflected sensations of extreme delight. Our constant care must be to secure that they do look, and listen, touch, and smell; and the way to this is by sympathetic action on our part: what we look at they will look at; the odours we perceive, they, too, will get" (Vol. 2, pp. 192, 193).

8. Don't feel that you must do an exhaustive study of each object.

"In the first place, it is unnecessary in the family to give an exhaustive examination to every object; one quality might be discussed in this, another quality in that" (Vol. 2, p. 183).

9. Use objects to informally teach your child the concept and vocabulary of comparisons.

"We eat our bread and milk, and notice that bread is absorbent; and we overhaul our experience to discover other things which we know to be absorbent also; and we do what we can to compare these things as to whether they are less absorbent or more absorbent than bread. This is exceedingly important: the unobservant person states that an object is light, and considers that he has stated an ultimate fact: the observant person makes the same statement, but has in his mind a relative scale, and his judgment is of the more value because he compares, silently, with a series of substances to which this is relatively light.

"It is important that children should learn to recognise that high, low, sweet, bitter, long, short, agreeable, etc., etc., are comparative terms; while square, round, black, white, are positive terms, the application of which is not affected by comparison with other objects" (Vol. 2, p. 183).

"Care in this matter makes for higher moral, as well as intellectual development: half the dissensions in the world arise from an indiscriminate use of epithets" (Vol. 2, p. 184).

10. Use objects and everyday events to informally teach your child about weight.

" 'Would you say your bread (at dinner) was light or heavy?' The child would probably answer, 'Rather light.' 'Yes, we can only say that a thing is light by comparing it with others; what is bread light compared with?' 'A stone, a piece of coal, of cheese, of butter of the same size.' 'But it is heavy compared with?' 'A piece of sponge cake, a piece of sponge, of cork, of pumice,' and so on. 'What do you think it weighs?' 'An ounce,' 'an ounce and a half.' 'We'll try after dinner; you had better have another piece and save it,' and the weighing after dinner is a delightful operation. The power of judging of weight is worth cultivating. We heard the other

---

Notes

An epithet is a descriptive word or phrase.

"What we look at they will look at."

Using the Senses

Notes

Caeteris paribus *means "other things being equal."*

day of a gentleman who was required at a bazaar to guess the weight of a monster cake; he poised it and said it weighed eighteen pounds fourteen ounces, and it did exactly. *Caeteris paribus,* one has a greater respect for the man who made this accurate judgment than for the vague person, who suggested that the cake might weigh ten pounds.

"Letters, book parcels, an apple, an orange, a vegetable marrow, fifty things in the course of the day, give opportunities for this kind of object teaching; *i.e.* the practice of forming judgments as to the relative and absolute weight of objects by the irresistance, that is their opposition to our muscular force, perceived by our sense of touch. By degrees the children are trained to observe that the relative weights of objects depend upon their relative density, and are introduced to the fact that we have a standard of weight" (Vol. 2, pp. 184, 185).

11. Use objects and everyday events to informally teach your child about size.

"In the same way children should be taught to measure objects by the eye. How high is that candlestick? How long and broad that picture-frame? and so on—verifying their statements. What is the circumference of that bowl? of the clock-face? of that flower-bed? How tall is So-and-so, and So-and-so? How many hands high are the horses of their acquaintance? Divide a slip of wood, a sheet of paper into halves, thirds, quarters by the eye, lay a walking-stick at right angles with another; detect when a picture, curtain, etc., hangs out of the perpendicular. This sort of practice will secure for children what is called a correct, or true, eye" (Vol. 2, p. 185).

12. Use objects and everyday events to encourage your child to listen carefully.

"A quick and true ear is another possession that does not come by Nature, or anyway, if it does, it is too often lost. How many sounds can you distinguish in a sudden silence out of doors? Let these be named in order from the less to the more acute. Let the notes of the birds be distinguished, both call-notes and song-notes; the four or five distinct sounds to be heard in the flow of a brook. Cultivate accuracy in distinguishing footfalls and voices; in discerning, with their eyes shut, the direction from which a sound proceeds, in which footsteps are moving. Distinguish passing vehicles by the sounds; as lorry, brougham, dog-cart" (Vol. 2, p. 185).

13. Use everyday objects and events to encourage your child to sharpen his sense of smell.

"By the way, why is it that the baby does not exercise with purpose his organ of smell? He screws up a funny little nose when he is taught to sniff at a flower, but this is a mere trick; he does not naturally make experiments as to whether things are odorous, while each of his other senses affords him keen joy. No doubt the little nose is, involuntarily, very active; but can his inertness in this matter be a hereditary failing? It may be that we all allow ourselves to go about with obtuse nostrils. If so, this is a matter for the attention of mothers, who should bring up their children not only to receive, which is involuntary and vague, but to perceive odours from the first" (Vol. 2, p. 182).

"We do not attach enough importance to the discrimination of odours, whether

"Our constant care must be to secure that they do look, and listen, touch, and smell."

as a safeguard to health or as a source of pleasure. Half the people one knows have nostrils which register no difference between the atmosphere of a large, and so-called 'airy,' room, whose windows are never opened, and that of a room in which a through current of air is arranged for at frequent intervals: and yet health depends largely on delicate perception as regards the purity of the atmosphere. The odours which result in diphtheria or typhoid are perceptible, however slight, and a nose trained to detect the faintest malodorous particles in food, clothing, or dwelling, is to the possessor a safeguard from disease" (Vol. 2, p. 186).

"Every new odour perceived is a source, if not of warning, of recurrent satisfaction or interest. We are acquainted with too few of the odours which the spring-time offers. Only this spring the present writer learned two peculiarly delightful odours quite new to her, that of young larch twigs, which have much the same kind and degree of fragrance as the flower of the syringa, and the pleasant musky aroma of a box-hedge. Children should be trained to shut their eyes, for example, when they come into the drawing-room, and discover by their nostrils what odorous flowers are present; should discriminate the garden odours let loose by a shower of rain" (Vol. 2, pp. 186, 187).

14. Encourage your child to cultivate his sense of taste objectively rather than subjectively.

"We all recognise that the training of the senses is an important part of education. One caution is necessary: from the very first a child's sensations should be treated as matters of objective and not of subjective interest. Marmalade, for example, is interesting, not because it is 'nice'—a fact not to be dwelt upon at all—but because one can discern in it different flavours and the modifying effect of the oil secreted in the rind of the orange" (Vol. 2, pp. 179, 180).

"Flavour, again, offers a wide range for delicate discrimination. At first sight it would appear difficult to cultivate the sense of flavour without making a child more or less of a gourmand; but the fact is, that the strong flavours which titillate the palate destroy the power of perception. The young child who lives upon milk-foods has, probably, more pleasure in flavour than the diner-out who is familiar with the confections of a *cordon bleu*. At the same time, one would prefer to make flavour a source of interest rather than of sensuous pleasure to children: it is better that they should try to discern a flavour with their eyes shut, than that they should be allowed to think or say that things are 'nice' or 'nasty.' This sort of fastidiousness should be cried down. It is not well to make a child eat what he does not like, as that would only make him dislike that particular dish always; but to let him feel that he shows a want of self-control and manliness, when he expresses distaste for wholesome food, is likely to have a lasting effect" (Vol. 2, pp. 187, 188).

15. Sensory gymnastics, like those described above, will help your child cultivate good observation skills that will serve him well in the future.

"We have barely touched on the sorts of object-lessons, appealing now to one sense and now to another, which should come incidentally every day in the family. We are apt to regard an American Indian as a quite uneducated person; he is, on the contrary, highly educated in so far as that he is able to discriminate sensory

Notes

A gourmand is a person who appreciates good food.

A cordon bleu is a chef famous for his skill.

"From the very first a child's sensations should be treated as matters of objective and not of subjective interest."

Notes

See chapter 6 for more on making a personal acquaintance with nature.

impressions, and to take action upon these, in a way which is bewildering to the book-learned European. It would be well for parents to educate a child, for the first half-dozen years of his life, at any rate, on 'Red Indian' lines. Besides the few points we have mentioned, he should be able to discriminate colours and shades of colour; relative degrees of heat in woollen, wood, iron, marble, ice; should learn the use of the thermometer; should discriminate objects according to their degrees of hardness; should have a cultivated eye and touch for texture; should, in fact, be able to get as much information about an object from a few minutes' study as to its form, colour, texture, size, weight, qualities, parts, characteristics, as he could learn out of many pages of a printed book. We approach the subject by the avenue of the child's senses rather than by that of the objects to be studied, because just now we have in view the occasional test exercises, the purpose of which is to give thorough culture to the several senses. An acquaintance with Nature and natural objects is another thing, and is to be approached in a slightly different way. A boy who is observing a beetle does not consciously apply his several senses to the beetle, but lets the beetle take the initiative, which the boy reverently follows: but the boy who is in the habit of doing sensory daily gymnastics will learn a great deal more about the beetle than he who is not so trained" (Vol. 2, pp. 188, 189).

16. A combination of incidental sensory cultivation and intentional object lessons offers a good plan.

"Definite object-lessons differ from these incidental exercises in that an object is in a manner exhausted by each of the senses in turn, and every atom of information it will yield got out of it. A good plan is to make this sort of a lesson a game. Pass your object round—a piece of bread, for example—and let each child tell some fact that he discovers by touch; another round, by smell; again, by taste; and again, by sight. Children are most ingenious in this kind of game, and it affords opportunities to give them new words, as friable, elastic, when they really ask to be helped to express in a word some discovery they have made. Children learn in this way to think with exactitude, to distinguish between friable and brittle; and any common information that is offered to them in the course of these exercises becomes a possession for ever. A good game in the nature of an object-lesson, suitable for a birthday party, is to have a hundred objects arranged on a table, unknown to the children; then lead the little party into the room, allow them three minutes to look round the table; afterwards, when they have left the room, let them write or tell in a corner, the names of all the objects they recollect. Some children will easily get fifty or sixty.

"No doubt the best and happiest exercise of the senses springs out of a loving familiarity with the world of nature, but the sorts of gymnastics we have indicated render the perceptions more acute, and are greatly enjoyed by children" (Vol. 2, pp. 189, 190).

17. A child's vocabulary will blossom as he seeks for words to name and describe what he is experiencing with his senses.

"We older people, partly because of our maturer intellect, partly because of our defective education, get most of our knowledge through the medium of words. We set the child to learn in the same way, and find him dull and slow. Why? Because it is only with a few words in common use that he associates a definite meaning; all

"A good plan is to make this sort of a lesson a game."

the rest are no more to him than the vocables of a foreign tongue. But set him face to face with a *thing*, and he is twenty times as quick as you are in knowing all about it; knowledge of things flies to the mind of a child as steel filings to a magnet. And, *pari passu* with his knowledge of things, his vocabulary grows; for it is a law of the mind that what we know, we struggle to express. This fact accounts for many of the apparently aimless questions of children; they are in quest, not of knowledge, but of *words* to express the knowledge they have" (Vol. 1, pp. 67, 68).

18. Every natural object is part of a whole network of more objects and scientific concepts, so one discovery will lead to more.

"Now take up a natural object, it does not matter what, and you are studying one of a group, a member of a series; whatever knowledge you get about it is so much towards the *science* which includes all of its kind. Break off an elder twig in the spring; you notice a ring of wood round a centre of pith, and there you have at a glance a distinguishing character of a great division of the vegetable world. You pick up a pebble. Its edges are perfectly smooth and rounded: why? you ask. It is water-worn, weather-worn. And that little pebble brings you face to face with *disintegration*, the force to which, more than to any other, we owe the aspects of the world which we call *picturesque*—glen, ravine, valley, hill. It is not necessary that the child should be told anything about disintegration or dicotyledon, only that he should *observe* the wood and pith in the hazel twig, the pleasant roundness of the pebble; by-and-by he will learn the bearing of the facts with which he is already familiar—a very different thing from learning the reason why of facts which have never come under his notice" (Vol. 1, p. 70).

Questions to Ask about Using the Senses

- Do I realize that my child uses his five senses to learn about everything around him?
- Am I convinced that my child will learn at the right pace for him?
- Do I consider learning by using the five senses important and foundational to future learning?
- Am I allowing my child to work hard, but with no stress, by using his senses to examine new objects?
- Am I trying to put things worth observing in the path of my observant child?
- Do I present planned object lessons sparingly?
- Am I learning to recognize opportunities for everyday, on-the-spot, natural object lessons?
- Am I pointing out only one or two aspects of a natural object lesson?
- Am I trying to informally teach my child the concept and vocabulary of comparison?
- Am I using everyday opportunities to teach my child about weight?
- Do I look for informal everyday opportunities to teach my child about size?
- Am I encouraging my child to listen carefully?
- Am I seeking to informally help my child sharpen his sense of smell?
- Am I trying to help my child cultivate his sense of taste objectively rather than subjectively?

Notes

Pari passu *means "in an equal way."*

"This fact accounts for many of the apparently aimless questions of children; they are in quest, not of knowledge, but of *words* to express the knowledge they have."

- Do I believe that sensory activities like these will cultivate good observation skills in my child that will serve him well in the future?
- Am I including a combination of incidental sensory cultivation and intentional object lessons?
- Am I helping my child's vocabulary to blossom as he seeks for words to name and describe what he is experiencing with his senses?
- Do I understand how one natural object is part of a whole network of more objects and scientific concepts, so one discovery will lead to more?

More Quotes on Using the Senses

"Seeing, hearing and feeling are miracles, and each part and tag of me is a miracle."—Walt Whitman

"It is a golden maxim to cultivate the garden for the nose, and the eyes will take care of themselves."—Robert Louis Stevenson

"How good is man's life, the mere living! How fit to employ all the heart and the soul and the senses forever in joy!"—Robert Browning

"Of all the senses, sight must be the most delightful."—Helen Keller

"There are three schoolmasters for everybody that will employ them—the senses, intelligent companions, and books."—Henry Ward Beecher

"Smell is a potent wizard that transports you across thousands of miles and all the years you have lived."—Helen Keller

"We all recognise that the training of the senses is an important part of education."

Chapter 5
Outdoor Life

"In this time of extraordinary pressure, educational and social, perhaps a mother's first duty to her children is to secure for them a quiet growing time, a full six years of passive receptive life, the waking part of it spent for the most part out in the fresh air. And this, not for the gain in bodily health alone—body and soul, heart and mind, are nourished with food convenient for them when the children are let alone, let to live without friction and without stimulus amongst happy influences which incline them to be good" (Vol. 1, p. 43).

Charlotte's Basic Guidelines for Outdoor Life

1. Do not send your child outside, take him.

"In the first place, do not send them; if it is anyway possible, take them; for, although the children should be left much to themselves, there is a great deal to be done and a great deal to be prevented during these long hours in the open air" (Vol. 1, p. 43).

2. Whenever possible, spend hours outside.

"And long hours they should be; not two, but four, five, or six hours they should have on every tolerably fine day, from April till October. 'Impossible!' says an overwrought mother who sees her way to no more for her children than a daily hour or so on the pavements of the neighbouring London squares. Let me repeat, that I venture to suggest, not what is practicable in any household, but what seems to me *absolutely best for the children*; and that, in the faith that mothers work wonders once they are convinced that wonders are demanded of them. A journey of twenty minutes by rail or omnibus, and a luncheon basket, will make a day in the country possible to most town-dwellers; and if one day, why not many, even every suitable day?" (Vol. 1, pp. 43, 44).

"The claims of the schoolroom should not be allowed to encroach on the child's right to long hours daily for exercise and investigation" (Vol. 1, p. 177).

3. Maintain a balance between free exploration and intentional training during these hours outside.

"Supposing we have got them, what is to be done with these golden hours, so that every one shall be delightful? They must be spent with some method, or the mother will be taxed and the children bored. There is a great deal to be accomplished in this large fraction of the children's day. They must be kept in a joyous temper all the time, or they will miss some of the strengthening and refreshing held in charge for them by the blessed air. They must be let alone, left to themselves a great deal, to take in what they can of the beauty of earth and heavens; for of the evils of modern education few are worse than this—that the perpetual cackle of his elders leaves the

---

Notes

Charlotte recommended 4–6 hours outside every day, weather permitting, for children during the early years. However, keep in mind that the mothers to whom Charlotte was writing probably had household help with the laundry, cooking, and dishes. So don't feel guilty if you can't spend that much time outside. But do try to spend as much time as possible out in the fresh air.

"Mothers work wonders once they are convinced that wonders are demanded of them."

poor child not a moment of time, nor an inch of space, wherein to wonder—and grow. At the same time, here is the mother's opportunity to train the seeing eye, the hearing ear, and to drop seeds of truth into the open soul of the child, which shall germinate, blossom, and bear fruit, without further help or knowledge of hers" (Vol. 1, p. 44).

"The child, though under supervision, should be left much to himself—both that he may go to work in his own way on the ideas that he receives, and also that he may be the more open to natural influences" (Vol. 1, p. 178).

4. Also maintain a balance between exercise and resting times.

"Then, there is much to be got by perching in a tree or nestling in heather, but muscular development comes of more active ways, and an hour or two should be spent in vigorous play; and last, and truly least, a lesson or two must be got in" (Vol. 1, pp. 44, 45).

"Play, vigorous healthful play, is, in its turn, fully as important as lessons, as regards both bodily health and brain-power" (Vol. 1, p. 177).

5. Remember that it is not your business to entertain your child during the hours outside.

"Let us suppose mother and children arrived at some breezy open 'wherein it seemeth always afternoon.' In the first place, it is *not* her business to entertain the little people: there should be no story-books, no telling of tales, as little talk as possible, and that to some purpose. Who thinks to amuse children with tale or talk at a circus or pantomime? And here, is there not infinitely more displayed for their delectation?" (Vol. 1, p. 45).

6. Let the children first run free to use up their energy, then use some of the following Outdoor Activities.

"Our wise mother, arrived, first sends the children to let off their spirits in a wild scamper, with cry, hallo, and hullaballo, and any extravagance that comes into their young heads. There is no distinction between big and little; the latter love to follow in the wake of their elders, and, in lessons or play, to pick up and do according to their little might. As for the baby, he is in bliss: divested of his garments, he kicks and crawls, and clutches the grass, laughs soft baby laughter, and takes in his little knowledge of shapes and properties in his own wonderful fashion—clothed in a woollen gown, long and loose, which is none the worse for the worst usage it may get" (Vol. 1, p. 45).

Questions to Ask about Basic Guidelines for Outdoor Life

- Do I try to take my child outdoors as much as possible, rather than send him without me?
- Am I trying to spend hours outdoors?
- Am I seeking to maintain a balance between free exploration and intentional training during these hours outside?

- Am I also seeking to maintain a balance between exercise and resting times?
- Do I remember that it is not my business to entertain my child during those hours outdoors?
- Am I allowing my child to run free and use up energy first, then using some of the Outside Activities given in this chapter?

More Quotes on Outdoor Life

"It is not so much for its beauty that the forest makes a claim upon men's hearts, as for that subtle something, that quality of air that emanates from old trees, that so wonderfully changes and renews a weary spirit."—Robert Louis Stevenson

"A bear, however hard he tries, grows tubby without exercise."—A. A. Milne

"Leave all the afternoon for exercise and recreation, which are as necessary as reading. I will rather say more necessary because health is worth more than learning."—Thomas Jefferson

"To sit in the shade on a fine day and look upon verdure is the most perfect refreshment."—Jane Austen

"Just living is not enough . . . One must have sunshine, freedom, and a little flower."—Hans Christian Andersen

Meals Outdoors

1. Whenever possible, eat a meal outdoors.

"On fine days when it is warm enough to sit out with wraps, why should not tea and breakfast, everything but a hot dinner, be served out of doors? For we are an overwrought generation, running to nerves as a cabbage runs to seed; and every hour spent in the open is a clear gain, tending to the increase of brain power and bodily vigour, and to the lengthening of life itself. They who know what it is to have fevered skin and throbbing brain deliciously soothed by the cool touch of the air are inclined to make a new rule of life, 'Never be within doors when you can *rightly* be without' " (Vol. 1, p. 42).

2. Make outdoor meals joyous occasions.

"Besides the gain of an hour or two in the open air, there is this to be considered: meals taken *al fresco* are usually joyous, and there is nothing like gladness for converting meat and drink into healthy blood and tissue" (Vol. 1, pp. 42, 43).

3. Remember that your child is storing up memories of these outdoor meals for future enjoyment.

"All the time, too, the children are storing up memories of a happy childhood. Fifty years hence they will see the shadows of the boughs making patterns on the white tablecloth; and sunshine, children's laughter, hum of bees, and scent of flowers are being bottled up for after refreshment" (Vol. 1, p. 43).

"Meals taken *al fresco* are usually joyous."

Sight-Seeing

1. Make a game of careful observation.

"By-and-by the others come back to their mother, and, while wits are fresh and eyes keen, she sends them off on an exploring expedition—Who can see the most, and tell the most, about yonder hillock or brook, hedge, or copse. This is an exercise that delights children, and may be endlessly varied, carried on in the spirit of a game, and yet with the exactness and carefulness of a lesson" (Vol. 1, pp. 45, 46).

2. Allow your child to tell all he can recall about the destination explored.

" 'Find out all you can about that cottage at the foot of the hill; but do not pry about too much.' Soon they are back, and there is a crowd of excited faces, and a hubbub of tongues, and random observations are shot breathlessly into the mother's ear. 'There are bee-hives.' 'We saw a lot of bees going into one.' 'There is a long garden.' 'Yes, and there are sunflowers in it.' 'And hen-and-chicken daisies and pansies.' 'And there's a great deal of a pretty blue flower with rough leaves, mother; what do you suppose it is?' 'Borage for the bees, most likely; they are very fond of it.' 'Oh, and there are apple and pear and plum trees on one side; there's a little path up the middle, you know.' 'On which hand side are the fruit trees?' 'The right—no, the left; let me see, which is my thimble-hand? Yes, it is the right-hand side.' 'And there are potatoes and cabbages, and mint and things on the other side.' 'Where are the flowers, then?' 'Oh, they are just the borders, running down each side of the path.' 'But we have not told mother about the wonderful apple tree; I should think there are a million apples on it, all ripe and rosy!' 'A *million*, Fanny?' 'Well, a great many, mother; I don't know how many.' And so on, indefinitely; the mother getting by degrees a complete description of the cottage and its garden" (Vol. 1, p. 46).

3. Increase your child's vocabulary by giving him the name or word he is seeking for to complete the description of what he saw.

"This is all play to the children, but the mother is doing invaluable work; she is training their powers of observation and expression, increasing their vocabulary and their range of ideas by giving them the name and the uses of an object at the right moment,—when they ask, 'What is it?' and 'What is it for?' " (Vol. 1, pp. 46, 47).

4. Encourage your child in the habit of truthfulness by asking for careful facts without omission or exaggeration.

"And she is training her children in truthful habits, by making them careful to see the fact and to state it exactly, without omission or exaggeration. The child who describes, 'A tall tree, going up into a point, with rather roundish leaves; not a pleasant tree for shade, because the branches all go up,' deserves to learn the name of the tree, and anything her mother has to tell her about it. But the little bungler, who fails to make it clear whether he is describing an elm or a beech, should get no encouragement; not a foot should his mother move to see his tree, no coaxing should draw her into talk about it, until, in despair, he goes off, and comes back with some more certain note—rough or smooth bark, rough or smooth leaves,—

> "This is all play to the children, but the mother is doing invaluable work."

then the mother considers, pronounces, and, full of glee, he carries her off to see for herself" (Vol. 1, p. 47).

5. Keep your standards of careful observation high so your child will reap the benefits of accurate memories later in life.

"By degrees the children will learn *discriminatingly* every feature of the landscapes with which they are familiar; and think what a delightful possession for old age and middle life is a series of pictures imaged, feature by feature, in the sunny glow of the child's mind! The miserable thing about the childish recollections of most persons is that they are blurred, distorted, incomplete, no more pleasant to look upon than a fractured cup or a torn garment; and the reason is, not that the old scenes are forgotten, but that they were never fully *seen*. At the time, there was no more than a hazy impression that such and such objects were present, and naturally, after a lapse of years those features can rarely be recalled of which the child was not *cognisant* when he saw them before him" (Vol. 1, pp. 47, 48).

Picture-Painting

1. Encourage careful observation and accurate mental landscapes by playing the game of "picture-painting."

"So exceedingly delightful is this faculty of taking mental photographs, exact images, of the 'beauties of Nature' we go about the world for the refreshment of seeing, that it is worth while to exercise children in another way towards this end, bearing in mind, however, that they see the near and the minute, but can only be made with an effort to look at the wide and the distant" (Vol. 1, p. 48).

2. Introduce the game by describing a picture gallery in your mind with pictures that you can look at any time you want to.

"The children will delight in this game of 'picture-painting' all the more if the mother introduce it by describing some great picture-gallery she has seen—pictures of mountains, of moors, of stormy seas, of ploughed fields, of little children at play, of an old woman knitting,—and goes on to say, that though she does not paint her pictures on canvas and have them put in frames, she carries about with her just such a picture-gallery; for whenever she sees anything lovely or interesting, she looks at it until she has the picture in her 'mind's eye'; and then she carries it away with her, her own for ever, a picture 'on view' just when she wants it" (Vol. 1, pp. 49, 50).

3. Point out a landscape nearby and have your child "paint that picture" in his mind.

"Get the children to look well at some patch of landscape, and then to shut their eyes and call up the picture before them, if any bit of it is blurred, they had better look again. When they have a perfect image before their eyes, let them say what they see. Thus: 'I see a pond; it is shallow on this side, but deep on the other; trees come to the waters edge on that side, and you can see their green leaves and branches so plainly in the water that you would think there was a wood underneath. Almost touching the trees in the water is a bit of blue sky with a soft white cloud; and when

> "Get the children to look well at some patch of landscape, and then to shut their eyes and call up the picture before them."

you look up you see that same little cloud, but with a great deal of sky instead of a patch, because there are no trees up there. There are lovely little water-lilies round the far edge of the pond, and two or three of the big round leaves are turned up like sails. Near where I am standing three cows have come to drink, and one has got far into the water, nearly up to her neck,' etc." (Vol. 1, p. 48).

4. *If needed at first, point out some details in an interesting manner to draw your child's attention to them.*

"At first the children will want a little help in the art of seeing. The mother will say, 'Look at the reflection of the trees! There might be a wood under the water. What do those standing-up leaves remind you of?' and so on, until the children have noticed the salient points of the scene" (Vol. 1, p. 49).

5. *Give your child an example by describing a mental picture or two of your own.*

"She will even herself learn off two or three scenes, and describe them with closed eyes for the children's amusement; and such little mimics are they, and at the same time so sympathetic, that any graceful fanciful touch which she throws into her descriptions will be reproduced with variations in theirs" (Vol. 1, p. 49).

6. *Do picture-painting only occasionally, as it requires much effort to do correctly.*

"This, too, is an exercise children delight in, but, as it involves some strain on the attention, it is fatiguing, and should only be employed now and then. It is, however, well worth while to give children the habit of getting a bit of landscape by heart in this way, because it is the effort of recalling and reproducing that is fatiguing; while the altogether pleasurable act of seeing, *fully and in detail*, is likely to be repeated unconsciously until it becomes a habit by the child who is required now and then to reproduce what he sees" (Vol. 1, pp. 48, 49).

7. *Remember that you are investing in your child's future refreshment by helping him paint these pictures carefully in his mind's art gallery.*

"It would be difficult to overrate this habit of seeing and storing as a means of after-solace and refreshment. The busiest of us have holidays when we slip our necks out of the yoke and come face to face with Nature, to be healed and blessed by

'The breathing balm,
The silence and the calm
Of mute, insensate things.'

This immediate refreshment is open to everybody according to his measure; but it is a mistake to suppose that everybody is able to carry away a refreshing image of that which gives him delight. Only a few can say with Wordsworth, of scenes they have visited—

'Though absent long,
These forms of beauty have not been to me
As is a landscape to a blind man's eye;
But oft, in lonely rooms, and 'mid the din
Of towns and cities, I have owed to them,

> In hours of weariness, sensations sweet,
> Felt in the blood, and felt along the heart;
> And passing even into my purer mind,
> With tranquil restoration.'

And yet this is no high poetic gift which the rest of us must be content to admire, but a common reward for taking pains in the act of seeing which parents may do a great deal to confer upon their children" (Vol. 1, p. 50).

8. Be careful not to make your child's descriptions appear to be a feat of cleverness or a trick that he performs.

"The mother must beware how she spoils the simplicity, the *objective* character of the child's enjoyment, by treating his little descriptions as feats of cleverness to be repeated to his father or to visitors; she had better make a vow to suppress herself, 'to say nothing to nobody,' in his presence at any rate, though the child should show himself a born poet" (Vol. 1, pp. 50, 51).

Foreign Language Lesson

1. A short, ten-minute foreign-language lesson will offer a nice break in the day's activities.

"The bright hours fly by; and there is still at least one lesson on the programme, to say nothing of an hour or two for games in the afternoon. The thought of a *lesson* is uninviting after the discussion of much that is more interesting, and, truly, more important; but it need only be a little lesson, ten minutes long, and the slight break and the effort of attention will give the greater zest to the pleasure and leisure to follow" (Vol. 1, p. 80).

2. Teach your young child a foreign language orally, by listening to and repeating a few words and phrases daily in your selected language.

"The daily French lesson is that which should not be omitted. That children should learn French *orally*, by listening to and repeating French words and phrases; that they should begin so young that the difference of accent does not strike them, but they repeat the new French word all the same as if it were English and use it as freely; that they should learn a few—two or three, five or six—new French words daily, and that, at the same time, the old words should be kept in use—are points to be considered more fully hereafter" (Vol. 1, p. 80).

"As regards French, for instance, our difficulties are twofold—the want of a vocabulary, and a certain awkwardness in producing unfamiliar sounds. It is evident that both these hindrances should be removed in early childhood. The child should never see French words in print until he has learned to say them with as much ease and readiness as if they were English" (Vol. 1, p. 301).

3. Use the outdoor setting as the basis for your choice of words and phrases to teach.

"The French lesson may, however, be made to fit in with the spirit of the other

Notes

Charlotte taught French to her students. That foreign language was an obvious choice because of England's close proximity to France and the frequent French-speaking people the children would come in contact with. Your choice of foreign language may be different, but the principles of how to teach a foreign language can still apply.

"Children should learn French *orally*, by listening to and repeating French words and phrases."

Outdoor Life

Notes

out-of-door occupations; the half-dozen words may be the parts—leaves, branches, bark, trunk of a tree, or the colours of the flowers, or the movements of bird, cloud, lamb, child; in fact, the new French words should be but another form of expression for the ideas that for the time fill the child's mind" (Vol. 1, p. 81).

Outdoor Games

1. If the babies and toddlers wear out, allow them to take their naps outside.

"The afternoon's games, after luncheon, are an important part of the day's doings for the elder children, though the younger have probably worn themselves out by this time with the ceaseless restlessness by means of which Nature provides for the due development of muscular tissue in them; let them sleep in the sweet air, and awake refreshed" (Vol. 1, p. 81).

2. Encourage your child to exercise his lungs, as well as his body, outside where he won't disturb anyone.

"Meanwhile, the elders play; the more they run, and shout, and toss their arms, the more healthful is the play. And this is one reason why mothers should carry their children off to lonely places, where they may use their lungs to their hearts' content without risk of annoying anybody. The *muscular* structure of the organs of voice is not enough considered; children love to indulge in cries and shouts and view-halloos, and this 'rude' and 'noisy' play, with which their elders have not much patience, is no more than Nature's way of providing for the due exercise of organs, upon whose working power the health and happiness of the child's future largely depend. People talk of 'weak lungs,' 'weak chest,' 'weak throat,' but perhaps it does not occur to everybody that strong lungs and strong throat are commonly to be had on the same terms as a strong arm or wrist—by exercise, training, *use*, work" (Vol. 1, p. 81).

A Ronde *is a "round dance" in which the participants dance in a circle.*

3. Teach your children some fun singing games with which they can exercise body and lungs.

"Still, if the children can 'give voice' musically, and more rhythmically to the sound of their own voices, so much the better. In this respect French children are better off than English; they dance and sing through a hundred roundelays—just such games, no doubt, mimic marryings and buryings, as the children played at long ago in the market-place of Jerusalem.

"Before Puritan innovations made us a staid and circumspect people, English lads and lasses of all ages danced out little dramas on the village green, accompanying themselves with the words and airs of just such *rondes* as the French children sing to-day. We have a few of them left still—to be heard at Sunday-school treats and other gatherings of the children,—and they are well worth preserving: 'There came three dukes a-riding, a-riding, a-riding'; 'Oranges and lemons, say the bells of St. Clement's'; 'Here we come gathering nuts in May'; 'What has my poor prisoner done?' and many more, all set to delightful sing-song airs that little feet trip to merrily, the more so for the pleasant titillation of the words—dukes, nuts, oranges,—who could not go to the tune of such ideas?" (Vol. 1, p. 82).

"The afternoon's games, after luncheon, are an important part of the day's doings."

4. Select interesting singing games that have withstood the test of time, not just simple little sayings used in many kindergartens and preschools today.

"The promoters of the kindergarten system have done much to introduce games of this, or rather of a more educational kind; but is it not a fact that the singing games of the kindergarten are apt to be somewhat inane? Also, it is doubtful how far the prettiest plays, learnt at school and from a teacher, will take hold of the children as do the games which have been passed on from hand to hand through an endless chain of children, and are not to be found in the print-books at all" (Vol. 1, p. 82).

5. Encourage romping games such as races, chase, tag, follow the leader, playing with a ball or shuttlecock, or skipping rope.

"Cricket, tennis, and rounders are *the* games *par excellence* if the children are old enough to play them, both as giving free harmonious play to the muscles, and also as serving the highest moral purpose of games in bringing the children under the discipline of rules; but the little family we have in view, all of them under nine, will hardly be up to scientific games. Races and chases, 'tig,' 'follow my leader,' and any romping game they may invent, will be more to their minds: still better are the hoop, the ball, the shuttlecock, and the invaluable skipping-rope" (Vol. 1, p. 83).

Tig is also called "Tag."

6. Teach your child to skip rope backwards.

"For the rope, the very best use is for each child to skip with her own, throwing it *backwards* rather than forwards, so that the tendency of the movement is to expand the chest" (Vol. 1, p. 83).

7. Keep a family record of best scores on the shuttlecock to motivate mastery of the toy.

"Shuttlecock is a fine game, affording scope for ambition and emulation. Her biographer thinks it worth telling that Miss Austen could keep up in 'cup and ball' over a hundred times, to the admiration of nephews and nieces; in like manner, any feat in keeping up the shuttle-cock might be noted down as a family event, so that the children may be fired with ambition to excel in a game which affords most graceful and vigorous play to almost every muscle of the upper part of the body, and has this great recommendation, that it can be as well played within doors as without" (Vol. 1, p. 83).

A shuttlecock is like a "birdie" used in badminton. The game is played by using battledores, or small rackets, to bat the shuttlecock from one to the other as many times as possible without its touching the ground.

8. Challenge your child to learn to do shuttlecock with both hands simultaneously.

"Quite the best play is to keep up the shuttlecock with a battledore in each hand, so that the muscles on either side are brought equally into play" (Vol. 1, p. 83).

Miss Austen refers to Jane Austen, author of Pride and Prejudice, Sense and Sensibility, *and other classics.*

9. Keep on the lookout for new children's games to introduce to your family.

"But to 'ordain' about children's games is an idle waste of words, for here fashion is as supreme and as arbitrary as in questions of bonnet or crinoline" (Vol. 1, p. 83).

"The more they run, and shout, and toss their arms, the more healthful is the play."

Outdoor Life

Notes

10. Encourage your child to climb; it is great exercise.

"Climbing is an amusement not much in favour with mothers; torn garments, bleeding knees, and boot-toes rubbed into holes, to say nothing of more serious risks, make a strong case against this form of delight. But, truly, the exercise is so admirable—the body being thrown into endless graceful postures which bring every muscle into play,—and the training in pluck, daring, and resource so invaluable, that it is a pity trees and cliffs and walls should be forbidden even to little girls" (Vol. 1, pp. 83, 84).

11. Give your younger child opportunities to do small feats of climbing in order to get accustomed to what he is capable of.

"The mother may do a good deal to avert serious mishaps by accustoming the younger children to small feats of leaping and climbing, so that they learn, at the same time, courage and caution from their own experiences, and are less likely to follow the lead of too-daring playmates" (Vol. 1, p. 84).

12. Be careful not to startle your climbing child.

"Later, the mother had best make up her mind to share the feelings of the hen that hatched a brood of ducklings, remembering that a little scream, a sharp and sudden 'Come down instantly!' 'Tommy, you'll break your neck!' gives the child a nervous shock, and is likely to cause the fall it was meant to hinder by startling Tommy out of all presence of mind" (Vol. 1, p. 84).

13. Boating and swimming are also great outdoor exercises.

"Even boating and swimming are not without the reach of town-bred children, in days when everybody goes for a summer outing to the neighbourhood of the sea or of inland waters; and then, there are swimming-baths in most towns. It would be well if most children of seven were taught to swim, not only for the possible usefulness of the art, but as giving them an added means of motion, and, therefore, of delight" (Vol. 1, p. 84).

Outdoors in Winter

1. Take your child outside during winter months as well as summer months.

"All we have said hitherto applies to the summer weather, which is, alas for us! a very limited and uncertain quantity in our part of the world. The question of out-of-door exercise in winter and in wet weather is really more important; for who that could would not be abroad in the summer time? If the children are to have what is quite the best thing for them, they should be two or three hours every day in the open air all through the winter, say an hour and a half in the morning and as long in the afternoon" (Vol. 1, p. 85).

2. Encourage fun winter activities such as sliding, snow-balling, and snow-building.

"When frost and snow are on the ground children have very festive times, what

"The mother may do a good deal to avert serious mishaps by accustoming the younger children to small feats of leaping and climbing."

with sliding, snow-balling, and snow-building" (Vol. 1, p. 85).

3. Do your best to keep your child interested in outdoor objects even during gray winter days.

"But even on the frequent days when it is dirty under foot and dull over head they should be kept interested and alert, so that the heart may do its work cheerfully, and a grateful glow be kept up throughout the body in spite of clouds and cold weather" (Vol. 1, p. 85).

4. Use fun shop windows to cultivate the habit of attention during winter walks.

"Winter walks, too, whether in town or country, give great opportunities for cultivating the habit of attention. The famous conjurer, Robert Houdin, relates in his autobiography, that he and his son would pass rapidly before a shop window, that of a toy-shop, for instance, and each cast an attentive glance upon it. A few steps further on each drew paper and pencil from his pocket, and tried which could enumerate the greater number of the objects momentarily seen in passing. The boy surprised his father in quickness of apprehension, being often able to write down forty objects, whilst his father could scarcely reach thirty; yet on their returning to verify his statement, the son was rarely found to have made a mistake. Here is a hint for a highly educational amusement for many a winter's walk" (Vol. 1, pp. 86, 87).

Outdoor Geography

1. Teach your child basic concepts in geography during your hours outdoors by following these progressive instructions.

"The child gets his rudimentary notions of geography as he gets his first notions of natural science, in those long hours out of doors of which we have already seen the importance" (Vol. 1, p. 273).

2. Use what is known to give an idea of the unknown.

"The mother, who knows better, will find a hundred opportunities to teach geography by the way: a duck-pond is a lake or an inland sea; any brooklet will serve to illustrate the great rivers of the world; a hillock grows into a mountain—an Alpine system; a hazel-copse suggests the mighty forests of the Amazon; a reedy swamp, the rice-fields of China; a meadow, the boundless prairies of the West; the pretty purple flowers of the common mallow is a text whereon to hang the cotton fields of the Southern States: indeed, the whole field of pictorial geography—maps may wait until by-and-by—may be covered in this way" (Vol. 1, p. 72).

3. Observe the position of the sun and how it tells the time of day.

"The children should be taught to observe the position of the sun in the heavens from hour to hour, and by his position, to tell the time of day. Of course they will want to know why the sun is such an indefatigable traveller, and thereby hangs a

Notes

Keep in mind that Charlotte lived in England, where the winter weather may be vastly different from the area in which you live. Use wisdom, but not excuses, in your decisions about being outside during winter days.

"The mother, who knows better, will find a hundred opportunities to teach geography by the way."

Notes

Remember that the instructions given in Volume 1, and presented here, are for children through age 9. Don't be in a hurry to get through all the geography concepts. Move at your child's pace. Charlotte explained: "for educative purposes, the child must learn such geography, and in such a way, that his mind shall thereby be stored with ideas, his imagination with images; for practical purposes he must learn such geography only as, the nature of his mind considered, he will be able to remember; in other words, he must learn what interests him" *(Vol. 1, p. 273).*

" 'Clouds and rain, snow and hail, winds and vapours, fulfilling His word'—are all everyday mysteries that the mother will be called upon to explain faithfully, however simply."

wonderful tale, which they may as well learn in the 'age of faith,' of the relative sizes of sun and earth, and of the nature and movements of the latter" (Vol. 1, p. 73).

4. Prepare simple yet accurate explanations of clouds, rain, snow, and hail to give your child when he asks about them.

" 'Clouds and rain, snow and hail, winds and vapours, fulfilling His word'—are all everyday mysteries that the mother will be called upon to explain faithfully, however simply" (Vol. 1, p. 73).

5. Teach distance first by the number of paces between locations, then move to measurements.

"There are certain ideas which children must get from within a walking radius of their own home if ever they are to have a real understanding of maps and of geographical terms.

"Distance is one of these, and the first idea of distance is to be attained by what children find a delightful operation. A child walks at his usual pace; somebody measures and tells him the length of his pace, and then he measures the paces of his brothers and sisters. Then such a walk, such a distance, here and there, is solemnly paced, and a little sum follows—so many inches or feet covered by each pace equals so many yards in the whole distance. Various short distances about the child's home should be measured in this way" (Vol. 1, p. 73).

6. Next add the concept of the time it takes to cover a distance.

"And when the idea of covering distance is fully established, the idea of time as a means of measurement should be introduced. The time taken to pace a hundred yards should be noted down. Having found out that it takes two minutes to pace a hundred yards, children will be able for the next step—that if they have walked for thirty minutes, the walk should measure fifteen hundred yards; in thirty-five minutes they would have walked a mile, or rather seventeen hundred and fifty yards, and then they could add the ten yards more which would make a mile. The longer the legs the longer the pace, and most grown people can walk a mile in twenty minutes" (Vol. 1, pp. 73, 74).

7. After your child is familiar with distance, introduce the idea of direction by first observing the progress of the sun.

"By the time they have got somewhat familiar with the idea of distance, that of *direction* should be introduced. The first step is to make children observant of the progress of the sun. The child who observes the sun for a year and notes down for himself, or dictates, the times of his rising and setting for the greater part of the year, and the points of his rising and setting, will have secured a basis for a good deal of definite knowledge. Such observation should take in the reflection of the sun's light, the evening light reflected by east windows, the morning light by west windows; the varying length and intensity of shadows, the cause of shadows, to be learned by the shadow cast by a figure between the blind and a candle. He should associate, too, the hot hours of the day with the sun high overhead, and the cool hours of the morning and evening with a low sun; and should be reminded, that if he stands straight before the fire, he feels the heat more than if he were in a corner of the room. When he is prepared by a little observation in the course of the sun, he is ready to take in the idea of direction, which depends entirely upon the sun" (Vol. 1, p. 74).

8. Next introduce east, west, north, and south as they relate to the sun's progress through the sky.

"Of course the first two ideas are that the sun rises in the east and sets in the west; from this fact he will be able to tell the direction in which the places near his own home, or the streets of his own town, lie. Bid him stand so that his right is towards the east where the sun rises, and his left towards the west where the sun sets. Then he is looking towards the north and his back is towards the south. All the houses, streets and towns on his right hand are to the east of him, those on the left are to the west. The places he must walk straight forward to reach are north of him, and the places behind him are to the south. If he is in a place new to him where he has never seen the sun rise or set and wants to know in what direction a certain road runs, he must notice in what direction his own shadow falls at twelve o'clock, because at noon the shadows of all objects fall towards the north. Then if he face the north, he has, as before, the south behind him, the east on his right hand, the west on his left; or if he face the sun at noon, he faces south" (Vol. 1, pp. 74, 75).

9. Encourage your child to practice finding the directions of nearby locations.

"This will throw an interesting light for him on the names of our great railways. A child may become ready in noticing the directions of places by a little practice. Let him notice how each of the windows of his schoolroom faces, or the windows of each of the rooms in his home; the rows of houses he passes in his walks, and which are north, south, east and west sides of the churches he knows" (Vol. 1, p. 75).

10. Help your child identify the wind's direction.

"He will soon be prepared to notice the direction of the wind by noticing the smoke from the chimneys, the movement of branches, corn, grass, etc. If the wind blow from the north—'The north wind doth blow and we shall have snow.' If it blow from the west, a west wind, we expect rain. Care must be taken at this point to make it clear to the child that the wind is named after the quarter it comes from, and not from the point it blows towards—just as he is English because he was born in England, and not French because he goes to France" (Vol. 1, pp. 75, 76).

11. Next combine the ideas of distance and direction.

"The ideas of distance and direction may now be combined. Such a building is two hundred yards to the east of the gate, such a village two miles to the west. He will soon come across the difficulty, that a place is not exactly east or west, north or south. It is well to let him give, in a round-about way, the direction of places as—'more to the east than the west,' 'very near the east but not quite,' 'half-way between east and west.' He will value the exact means of expression all the more for having felt the need of them" (Vol. 1, p. 76).

12. Once he understands direction, give your child a compass and help him practice using it.

"Later, he should be introduced to the wonders of the mariner's compass, should

> "A child may become ready in noticing the directions of places by a little practice."

have a little pocket compass of his own, and should observe the four cardinal and all other points. These will afford him the names for directions that he has found it difficult to describe.

"Then he should do certain compass drills in this way: Bid him hold the N of the compass towards the north. 'Then, with the compass in your hand, turn towards the east, and you will see a remarkable thing. The little needle moves, too, but moves quite by itself in just the other direction. Turn to the west, and again the needle moves in the opposite direction to that in which you move. However little you turn, a little quiver of the needle follows your movement. And you look at it, wondering how the little thing could perceive you had moved, when you hardly knew it yourself. Walk straight on in any direction, and the needle is fairly steady; only fairly steady, because you are sure, without intending it, to move a little to the right or left. Turn round very slowly, a little bit at a time, beginning at the north and turning towards the east, and you may make the needle also move round in a circle. It moves in the opposite direction to yourself, for it is trying to get back to the north from which you are turning' " (Vol. 1, pp. 76, 77).

13. Introduce the concept of boundaries using nearby locations and examples.

"The children having got the idea of direction, it will be quite easy to introduce that of boundaries—such and such a turnip field, for instance, is bounded by the highroad on the south, by a wheat crop on the south-east, a hedge on the north-east, and so on; the children getting by degrees the idea that the boundaries of a given space are simply whatever touches it on every side. Thus one crop may touch another without any dividing line, and therefore one crop bounds the other. It is well that children should get clear notions on this subject, or, later, they will be vague when they learn that such a county is 'bounded' by so and so" (Vol. 1, p. 77).

14. Encourage your child to identify what is unique about each area that has boundaries around it.

"In connection with bounded spaces, whether they be villages, towns, ponds, fields, or what not, children should be led to notice the various crops raised in the district, why pasture-lands and why cornfields, what manner of rocks appear, and how many sorts of tree grow in the neighbourhood" (Vol. 1, p. 77).

15. Next help your child draw a map of certain boundaries in the sand, and gradually help him determine how to draw a map to scale.

"He gets his first notions of a map from a rude sketch, a mere few lines and dots, done with pencil and paper, or, better still, with a stick in the sand or gravel" (Vol. 1, p. 274).

"For every field or other space that is examined, they should draw a rude plan in the sand, giving the shape roughly and lettering the directions as N, S, W, etc.

"By-and-by, when they have learned to draw plans indoors, they will occasionally pace the length of a field and draw their plan according to scale, allowing an inch for five or for ten yards. The ground-plans of garden, stables, house, etc., might follow" (Vol. 1, p. 77).

16. In the end, he can draw a map of his neighborhood, incorporating all the geographical concepts that he has learned.

"It is probable that a child's own neighbourhood will give him opportunities to learn the meaning of hill and dale, pool and brook, watershed, the current, bed, banks, tributaries of a brook, the relative positions of villages and towns; and all this local geography he must be able to figure roughly on a plan done with chalk on a rock, or with walking-stick in the gravel, perceiving the relative distances and situations of the places he marks" (Vol. 1, p. 78).

17. Natural geography knowledge whets the appetite to continue learning about places far and near.

"By the time he is seven, or before, he finds himself in need of further knowledge. He has read of hot countries and cold countries, has observed the seasons and the rising and setting of the sun, has said to himself—

'Twinkle, twinkle, little star,
How I wonder what you are!'—

knows something of ocean and sea, has watched the tide come in and go out, has seen many rough sketch-maps made and has made some for himself, and has, no doubt, noticed the criss-cross lines on a 'proper' map; that is to say, his mind is prepared for knowledge in various directions; there are a number of things concerned with geography which he really wants to know" (Vol. 1, p. 277).

"His mind is prepared for knowledge in various directions."

Chapter 6
Personal Acquaintance with Nature

Davy burst through the back door. "Mom, Mom! Did you see my oak tree this morning?" he called excitedly.

Susan set down the tea kettle and started walking in Davy's direction. She wanted to encourage his excitement about "his" tree, but she also wanted to keep his muddy boots on the back-door rug. "No, honey, I haven't seen it yet today. What's up?" she asked.

"It has buds on the branches! Real buds! Come look!" And he was back out the door before she could reply.

Susan chuckled as her little boy disappeared around the corner. Quickly she took a short detour, just long enough to grab their Firsts Calendar and set it on the table. *This will remind me to write the oak tree buds on the calendar when we get back.*

Then slipping her feet into her garden clogs, she hurried to join her son outdoors.

Charlotte's Thoughts on a Personal Acquaintance with Nature

1. Your young child should get to know the name, look, and behavior of every natural object that he has access to in its natural environment.

"There is no knowledge so appropriate to the early years of a child as that of the name and look and behaviour *in situ* of every natural object he can get at" (Vol. 1, p. 32).

"My object is to show that the chief function of the child—his business in the world during the first six or seven years of his life—is to find out all he can, about whatever comes under his notice, by means of his five senses; that he has an insatiable appetite for knowledge got in this way; and that, therefore, the endeavour of his parents should be to put him in the way of making acquaintance freely with Nature and natural objects" (Vol. 1, p. 96).

"Intimate acquaintance with every natural object within his reach is the first, and, possibly, the best part of a child's education" (Vol. 2, p. 261).

"We make a great point of giving play to the intelligent curiosity of the children about all that lives and grows within their ken. For instance, I should think most of 'our' mothers would feel disgraced if her child of six were not able to recognise any ordinary British tree from a twig with *leaf-buds* only. It's Nature's lore, and the children take to it like ducks to the water; the first six or seven years of their lives are spent out of doors—in possible weather—learning this sort of thing, instead of pottering over picture-books and A B C" (Vol. 5, p. 166).

Notes

This chapter will tell you a little about doing nature study, focusing on preschool-age ideas. For a more in-depth collection of Charlotte's ideas on nature study, see Hours in the Out-of-Doors: A Charlotte Mason Nature Study Handbook *available from SimplyCharlotteMason.com*

In situ *means "in the place" and refers to natural habitat or environment.*

"Intimate acquaintance with every natural object within his reach is the first, and, possibly, the best part of a child's education."

Personal Acquaintance with Nature

Notes

The three R's are reading, writing, and 'rithmetic.

In situ means "in the place" and refers to natural habitat or environment.

"A love of Nature, implanted so early that it will seem to them hereafter to have been born in them, will enrich their lives with pure interests, absorbing pursuits, health, and good humour."

"Some children are born naturalists, with a bent inherited, perhaps, from an unknown ancestor; but every child has a natural interest in the living things about him which it is the business of his parents to encourage" (Vol. 1, p. 58).

"His parents know that the first step in intimacy is recognition; and they will measure his education, not solely by his progress in the 'three R's,' but by the number of living and growing things he knows by look, name, and habitat. A child of six will note with eager interest the order of time in which the trees put on their leaves; will tell you whether to look in hedge, or meadow, or copse, for eyebright, wood-sorrel, ground-ivy; will not think that flowers were made to be plucked, for—

' 'Tis (his) faith that every flower
Enjoys the air it breathes'—

but will take his friends to see where the milk-wort grows, or the bog-bean, or the sweet-gale. The birds of the air are no longer casual; he soon knows when and where to expect the redstart and the meadow pipit. The water-skater and the dragon-fly are interesting and admired acquaintances. His eyes have sparkled at the beauty of crystals, and, though he may not have been able to find them *in situ*, he knows the look of the crystals of lime and quartz, and the lovely pink of felspar, and many more" (Vol. 3, pp. 76, 77).

2. A personal acquaintance with nature, encouraged from the start, will enrich your child's life.

"A love of Nature, implanted so early that it will seem to them hereafter to have been born in them, will enrich their lives with pure interests, absorbing pursuits, health, and good humour" (Vol. 1, p. 71).

"It would be well if all we persons in authority, parents and all who act for parents, could make up our minds that there is no sort of knowledge to be got in these early years so valuable to children as that which they get for themselves of the world they live in. Let them once get touch with Nature, and a habit is formed which will be a source of delight through life. We were all meant to be naturalists, each in his degree, and it is inexcusable to live in a world so full of the marvels of plant and animal life and to care for none of these things" (Vol. 1, p. 61).

"The boy who can tell you off-hand where to find each of the half-dozen most graceful birches, the three or four finest ash trees in the neighbourhood of his home, has chances in a life a dozen to one compared with the lower, slower intelligence that does not know an elm from an oak—not merely chances of success, but chances of a larger, happier life, for it is curious how certain *feelings* are linked with the mere observation of Nature and natural objects" (Vol. 1, p. 68).

3. A personal acquaintance with nature lays the foundation for science studies.

"There is no part of a child's education more important than that he should lay, by his own observation, a wide basis of *facts* towards scientific knowledge in the future. He must live hours daily in the open air, and, as far as possible, in the country; must look and touch and listen; must be quick to note, *consciously*, every peculiarity of habit or structure, in beast, bird, or insect; the manner of growth and fructification of every plant" (Vol. 1, p. 264).

"Many a man got his turn for natural science because as a boy he lived in the country, and had a chance to observe living things and their ways. Nobody took pains to develop his faculty; all he had was opportunity. If the boy's mind is crammed with other matters, he has no opportunity; and you may meet men of culture who have lived most of their lives in the country, and don't know a thrush from a blackbird" (Vol. 2, pp. 70, 71).

"Audubon, the American ornithologist, is another instance of the effect of this kind of early training. 'When I had hardly learned to walk,' he says, 'and to articulate those first words always so endearing to parents, the productions of Nature that lay spread all around were constantly pointed out to me. . . . My father generally accompanied my steps, procured birds and flowers for me, and pointed out the elegant movements of the former, the beauty and softness of their plumage, the manifestations of their pleasure, or their sense of danger, and the always perfect forms and splendid attire of the latter. He would speak of the departure and return of the birds with the season, describe their haunts, and, more wonderful than all, their change of livery, thus exciting me to study them, and to raise my mind towards their great Creator' " (Vol. 1, p. 59).

"It is infinitely well worth of the mother's while to take some pains every day to secure, in the first place, that her children spend hours daily amongst rural and natural objects; and, in the second place, to infuse into them, or rather, to cherish in them, the love of investigation" (Vol. 1, p. 71).

"That the child should be taken daily, if possible, to scenes—moor or meadow, park, common, or shore—where he may find new things to examine, and so add to his store of *real* knowledge. That the child's observation should be directed to flower or boulder, bird or tree; that, in fact, he should be employed in gathering the common information which is the basis of scientific knowledge" (Vol. 1, p. 177).

4. If possible, let your child observe farming and crops.

"In the course of this 'sight-seeing' and 'picture-painting,' opportunities will occur to make the children familiar with rural objects and employments. If there are farm-lands within reach, they should know meadow and pasture, clover, turnip, and corn field, under every aspect, from the ploughing of the land to the getting in of the crops" (Vol. 1, p. 51).

5. Look for wildflowers and take note of their locations for future sightings.

"Milkwort, eyebright, rest-harrow, lady's-bedstraw, willow-herb, every wild flower that grows in their neighbourhood, they should know quite well; should be able to describe the leaf—its shape, size, growing from the root or from the stem; the manner of flowering—a head of flowers, a single flower, a spike, etc. And, having made the acquaintance of a wild flower, so that they can never forget it or mistake it, they should examine the spot where they find it, so that they will know for the future in what sort of ground to look for such and such a flower. 'We should

---

Notes

Read more about sight-seeing and picture-painting in chapter 5, pages 58 and 59.

"It is infinitely well worth of the mother's while to take some pains every day to secure, in the first place, that her children spend hours daily amongst rural and natural objects; and, in the second place, to infuse into them, or rather to cherish in them, the love of investigation."

Personal Acquaintance with Nature

Notes

You can also use the Internet to help identify plants.

"Every common miracle which the child sees with his own eyes makes of him for the moment another Newton."

find wild thyme here!' 'Oh, this is the very spot for marsh marigolds; we must come here in the spring' " (Vol. 1, p. 51).

6. Use a field guide to help you identify your child's findings.

"If the mother is no great botanist, she will find Miss Ann Pratt's *Wild Flowers* very useful, with its coloured plates, like enough to identify the flowers by, common English names, and pleasant facts and fancies that the children delight in" (Vol. 1, p. 51).

7. Make a notebook of wildflowers by pressing, mounting, and labeling them, or have your child draw or paint them.

"To make collections of wild flowers for the several months, press them, and mount them neatly on squares of cartridge paper, with the English name, habitat, and date of finding of each, affords much happy occupation and, at the same time, much useful training: better still is it to accustom children to make careful brush drawings of the flowers that interest them, of the whole plant where possible" (Vol. 1, p. 52).

8. In the winter, adopt six or so trees to be year-long friends and follow them through the seasons.

"Children should be made early intimate with the trees, too; should pick out half a dozen trees, oak, elm, ash, beech, in their winter nakedness, and take these to be their year-long friends. In the winter, they will observe the light tresses of the birch, the knotted arms of the oak, the sturdy growth of the sycamore. They may wait to learn the names of the trees until the leaves come. By-and-by, as the spring advances, behold a general stiffening and look of life in the still bare branches; life stirs in the beautiful mystery of the leaf-buds, a nest of delicate baby-leaves lying in downy warmth within many waterproof wrappings; oak and elm, beech and birch, each has its own way of folding and packing its leaflets; observe the 'ruby-budded lime' and the ash, with its pretty stag's foot of a bud, not green but black—

'More black than ash-buds in the front of March' " (Vol. 1, p. 52).

"Presently they have the delight of discovering that the great trees have flowers, too, flowers very often of the same hue as their leaves, and that some trees have put off having their leaves until their flowers have come and gone. By-and-by there is the fruit, and the discovery that every tree—with exceptions which they need not learn yet—and every plant bears fruit, 'fruit and seed after his kind' " (Vol. 1, pp. 53, 54).

"The party come across a big tree which they judge, from its build, to be an oak—down it goes in the diary; and when the leaves are out, the children come again to see if they are right" (Vol. 1, p. 86).

9. Take note of the changes that come with the seasons.

"But it is hard to keep pace with the wonders that unfold themselves in 'the bountiful season, bland.' There are the dangling catkins and the little ruby-red pistil-late flowers of the hazel—clusters of flowers, both of them, two sorts on a single tree; and the downy staminate catkins of the willow; and the festive breaking out of all the trees into lovely leafage; the learning the patterns of the leaves as they come out, and the naming of the trees from this and other signs. Then the flowers come, each shut up tight in the dainty casket we call a bud, as cunningly wrapped as the leaves in their buds, but less carefully guarded, for these 'sweet nurslings' delay their coming for the most part until earth has a warm bed to offer, and the sun a kindly welcome" (Vol. 1, pp. 52, 53).

10. Don't let rain or winter weather deter you from taking a nature walk.

"There is no reason why the child's winter walk should not be as fertile in observations as the poet's; indeed, in one way, it is possible to see the more in winter, because the things to be seen do not crowd each other out" (Vol. 1, p. 86).

"But what about the wet days? The fact is, that rain, unless of the heaviest, does the children no harm at all if they are suitably clothed" (Vol. 1, p. 87).

"Keep a child active and happy in the rain, and he gets nothing but good from his walk" (Vol. 1, p. 88).

11. Share your child's excitement in each new discovery.

" 'Suppose,' says Leigh Hunt, 'suppose flowers themselves were new! Suppose they had just come into the world, a sweet reward for some new goodness. . . . . Imagine what we should feel when we saw the first lateral stem bearing off from the main one, and putting forth a leaf. How we should watch the leaf gradually unfolding its little graceful hand; then another, then another; then the main stalk rising and producing more; then one of them giving indications of the astonishing novelty—a bud! then this mysterious bud gradually unfolding like the leaf, amazing us, enchanting us, almost alarming us with delight, as if we knew not what enchantment were to ensue, till at length, in all its fairy beauty, and odorous voluptuousness, and mysterious elaboration of tender and living sculpture, shines forth the blushing flower.' The *flowers*, it is true, are not new; but the *children* are; and it is the fault of their elders if every new flower they come upon is not to them a *Picciola*, a mystery of beauty to be watched from day to day with unspeakable awe and delight" (Vol. 1, p. 53).

"All this is stale knowledge to older people, but one of the secrets of the educator is to present nothing as stale knowledge, but to put himself in the position of the child, and wonder and admire with him; for every common miracle which the child sees with his own eyes makes of him for the moment another Newton" (Vol. 1, p. 54).

12. Create a family calendar of "firsts."

"It is a capital plan for the children to keep a calendar—the first oak-leaf, the first tadpole, the first cowslip, the first catkin, the first ripe blackberries, where seen, and when. The next year they will know when and where to look out for their favourites, and will, every year, be in a condition to add new observations. Think of the zest and interest, the *object*, which such a practice will give to daily walks and little excursions. There is hardly a day when some friend may not be expected to hold a first 'At Home' " (Vol. 1, p. 54).

Notes

Picciola *refers to the plant that was nurutred and cherished by Charney in his prison. The story is told in* Fifty Famous Stories Retold *by James Baldwin.*

Isaac Newton (1642–1727) *is regarded by many as the greatest figure in the history of science.*

"The *flowers*, it is true, are not new; but the *children* are."

Personal Acquaintance with Nature

Notes

The book Hours in the Out-of-Doors *gives more specifics on the nature diary or notebook.*

13. Older children may keep nature diaries.

"As soon as he is able to keep it himself, a nature-diary is a source of delight to a child. Every day's walk gives him something to enter: three squirrels in a larch tree, a jay flying across such a field, a caterpillar climbing up a nettle, a snail eating a cabbage leaf, a spider dropping suddenly to the ground, where he found ground ivy, how it was growing and what plants were growing with it, how bindweed or ivy manages to climb. Innumerable matters to record occur to the intelligent child. While he is quite young (five or six), he should begin to illustrate his notes freely with brush-drawings; he should have a little help at first in mixing colours, in the way of principles, not directions. He should not be told to use now this and now that, but, 'we get purple by mixing so and so,' and then he should be left to himself to get the right tint. As for drawing, instruction has no doubt its time and place; but his nature-diary should be left to his own initiative. A child of six will produce a dandelion, poppy, daisy, iris, with its leaves, impelled by the desire to represent what he sees, with surprising vigour and correctness.

"An exercise book with stiff covers serves for a nature-diary, but care is necessary in choosing paper that answers both for writing and brush-drawing" (Vol. 1, pp. 54, 55).

"Aesthetic appreciation follows close upon recognition, for does he not try from very early days to catch the flower in its beauty of colour and grace of gesture with his own paintbrush? The wise mother is careful to open her child's eyes to another kind of appreciation. She makes him look from a distance at a wild cherry-tree, or at a willow with its soft catkins, and she shows him that the picture on a Japanese screen has caught the very look of the thing, though when he comes to compare a single catkin or a single cherry blossom with those on the screen, there is no portraiture; and so he begins to learn at a very early age that to paint that which we see and that which we know to be there, are two different things, and that the former art is the more gratifying" (Vol. 3, p. 77).

14. Look for animals and insects—squirrels, rabbits, tadpoles, frogs, ants, bees, whatever you can find.

"Then, as for the 'living creatures,' here is a field of unbounded interest and delight. The domesticated animals are soon taken into kindly fellowship by the little people. Perhaps they live too far from the 'real country' for squirrels and wild rabbits to be more to them than a dream of possible delights. But surely there is a pond within reach—by road or rail—where tadpoles may be caught, and carried home in a bottle, fed, and watched through all their changes—fins disappearing, tails getting shorter and shorter, until at last there is no tail at all, and a pretty pert little frog looks you in the face. Turn up any chance stone, and you may come upon a colony of ants. We have always known that it becomes us to consider their ways and be wise; but now, think of all Lord Avebury has told us to make that twelve-year-old ant of his acquaintance quite a personage. Then, there are the bees. Some of us may have heard the late Dean Farrar describe that lesson he was present at, on 'How doth the little busy bee'—the teacher bright, but the children not responsive; they took no interest at all in little busy bees. He suspected the reason, and questioning the class, found that not one of them had ever seen a bee. 'Had never seen a bee! Think for a moment,' said he, 'of how much that implies'; and

"As soon as he is able to keep it himself, a nature-diary is a source of delight to a child."

then we were moved by an eloquent picture of the sad child-life from which bees and birds and flowers are all shut out. But how many children are there who do not live in the slums of London, and yet are unable to distinguish a bee from a wasp, or even a 'humble' from a honey-bee!" (Vol. 1, pp. 56, 57).

"Town children may get a great deal of pleasure in watching the ways of sparrows—knowing little birds, and easily tamed by a dole of crumbs,—and their days out will bring them in the way of new acquaintances" (Vol. 1, p. 59).

"A fourth relation is to the dumb creation; a relation of intelligent comprehension as well as of kindness. Why should not each of us be on friendly terms with the 'inmates of his house and garden'? Every child longs for intimacy with the creatures about him; and—
   'He prayeth best, who loveth best
      All things both great and small;
   For the dear God who loveth us,
      He made and loveth all' " (Vol. 3, p. 80).

15. Encourage your child to watch the animal, patiently and quietly.

"Children should be encouraged to *watch*, patiently and quietly, until they learn something of the habits and history of bee, ant, wasp, spider, hairy caterpillar, dragon-fly, and whatever of larger growth comes in their way. 'The creatures never have any habits while I am looking!' a little girl in some story-book is made to complain; but that was her fault; the bright keen eyes with which children are blest were made to see, and see into, the doings of creatures too small for the unaided observation of older people" (Vol. 1, p. 57).

16. Be careful not to allow your dislike of certain animals to discourage your child's love of nature.

"With regard to the horror which some children show of beetle, spider, worm, that is usually a trick picked up from grown-up people. Kingsley's children would run after their 'daddy' with a 'delicious worm,' a 'lovely toad,' a 'sweet beetle' carried tenderly in both hands. There are real antipathies not to be overcome, such as Kingsley's own horror of a spider; but children who are accustomed to hold and admire caterpillars and beetles from their babyhood will not give way to affected horrors. The child who spends an hour in watching the ways of some new 'grub' he has come upon will be a man of mark yet. Let all he finds out about it be entered in his diary—by his mother, if writing be a labour to him,—where he finds it, what it is doing, or seems to him to be doing; its colour, shape, legs: some day he will come across the name of the creature, and will recognise the description of an old friend" (Vol. 1, p. 58).

"Few children are equal to holding their own in the face of public opinion; and if they see that the things which interest them are indifferent or disgusting to you, their pleasure in them vanishes, and that chapter in the book of Nature is closed to them" (Vol. 1, p. 58).

Notes

"Consider their ways and be wise" refers to Proverbs 6:6–8.

Lord Avebury was John Lubbock (1834–1913), a British naturalist who wrote Ants, Bees, and Wasps.

Charles Kingsley (1819–1875) was an English clergyman and novelist.

"Children should be encouraged to *watch*, patiently and quietly, until they learn something of the habits and history of bee, ant, wasp, spider, hairy caterpillar, dragon-fly, and whatever of larger growth comes in their way."

17. Use nature books to encourage and expand what your child observes for himself.

"The real use of naturalists' books at this stage is to give the child delightful glimpses into the world of wonders he lives in, to reveal the sorts of things to be seen by curious eyes, and fill him with desire to make discoveries for himself" (Vol. 1, p. 64).

"The mother cannot devote herself too much to this kind of reading, not only that she may read tit-bits to her children about matters they have come across, but that she may be able to answer their queries and direct their observation. And not only the mother, but any woman, who is likely ever to spend an hour or two in the society of children, should make herself mistress of this sort of information; the children will adore her for knowing what they want to know, and who knows but she may give its bent for life to some young mind destined to do great things for the world" (Vol. 1, pp. 64, 65).

18. Only occasionally point out an especially beautiful landscape.

"There is one thing the mother will allow herself to do as interpreter between Nature and the child, but that not oftener than once a week or once a month, and with look and gesture of delight rather than with flow of improving words—she will point out to the child some touch of especial loveliness in colouring or grouping in the landscape or in the heavens" (Vol. 1, p. 79).

19. At times, point out God's creative touch in a natural object.

"One other thing she will do, but very rarely, and with tender filial reverence (most likely she will say her prayers, and speak out of her prayer, for to touch on this ground with *hard* words is to wound the soul of the child): she will point to some lovely flower or gracious tree, not only as a beautiful work, but a beautiful *thought* of God, in which we may believe He finds continual pleasure, and which He is pleased to see his human children rejoice in. Such a seed of sympathy with the Divine thought sown in the heart of the child is worth many of the sermons the man may listen to hereafter, much of the 'divinity' he may read" (Vol. 1, pp. 79, 80).

Questions to Ask about a Personal Acquaintance with Nature

- Am I providing opportunities for my child to get to know the name, look, and behavior of every natural object that he has access to in its natural environment?
- Do I believe that a personal acquaintance with nature, encouraged from the start, will enrich my child's life?
- Do I understand that a personal acquaintance with nature lays the foundation for science studies?
- Have I found an opportunity to let my child observe farming and crops?
- Do we look for wildflowers and take note of their locations for future sightings?

"If they see that the things which interest them are indifferent or disgusting to you, their pleasure in them vanishes, and that chapter in the book of Nature is closed to them."

- Do I have a field guide to help us identify my child's findings?
- Am I helping my child to make a notebook of wildflowers by pressing, mounting, and labeling them?
- Do I encourage my child to draw or paint wildflowers?
- Have we adopted six or so trees in the winter to be year-long friends and followed them through the seasons?
- Am I encouraging my child to take note of the changes that come with the seasons?
- Am I trying not to let rain or winter weather deter us from taking a nature walk?
- Do I seek to share my child's excitement in each new discovery?
- Are we keeping a family calendar of "firsts"?
- Am I helping my older child to keep a nature diary of his own?
- Do we look for animals and insects of all kinds?
- Am I encouraging my child to watch the animals, patiently and quietly?
- Am I trying not to allow my dislike of certain animals to discourage my child's love of nature?
- Are we reading nature books to encourage and expand what my child observes for himself?
- Do I occasionally point out an especially beautiful landscape?
- Do I try to point out God's creative touch in a natural object?

More Quotes on a Personal Acquaintance with Nature

"Reading about nature is fine, but if a person walks in the woods and listens carefully, he can learn more than what is in books, for they speak with the voice of God."—George Washington Carver

"Go forth under the open sky, and list To Nature's teachings."—William Cullen Bryant

"Nature is a good name for an effect whose cause is God."—William Cowper

"For in the true nature of things, if we rightly consider, every green tree is far more glorious than if it were made of gold and silver."—Martin Luther

"I perhaps owe having become a painter to flowers."—Claude Monet

"Consider the lilies how they grow: they toil not, they spin not; and yet I say unto you, that Solomon in all his glory was not arrayed like one of these."—Luke 12:27

"I frequently tramped eight or ten miles through the deepest snow to keep an appointment with a beech-tree, or a yellow birch, or an old acquaintance among the pines."—Henry David Thoreau

"Earth, with her thousand voices, praises God."—Samuel Taylor Coleridge

"Give the child delightful glimpses into the world of wonders he lives in."

Chapter 7
Play

Meagan came through the kitchen doorway and spotted her three-year-old perched on an overturned plastic toy crate that was sitting a bit precariously on top of a folding chair.

"Mom!" her five-year-old exclaimed. "Look! We're playing Little House. This is our covered wagon."

Both girls beamed up at Meagan, who couldn't help smiling back. "Very nice," she encouraged them.

"Oh!" The five-year-old spread her arms dramatically. "We need reins for the horses!"

Both girls scampered out of the room to look for reins. And Meagan took the opportunity to adjust the "covered wagon seat" and make it a little more stable.

Charlotte's Thoughts on Play

1. Children should have time for free play.

"There is a little danger in these days of much educational effort that children's play should be crowded out, or, what is from our present point of view the same thing, should be prescribed for and arranged until there is no more freedom of choice about play than that about work" (Vol. 3, p. 36).

"Play, vigorous healthful play, is, in its turn, fully as important as lessons, as regards both bodily health and brain-power" (Vol. 1, p. 177).

"The little child, indeed, is made happy day after day with spade and bucket, but that is because his unjaded imagination works without spur, and he is able to fill his sunny hours with glad interest, to make some ever new—
      'Little plan or chart,
  Some fragment of his dream of human life,
  Shaped by himself with newly-learned art' " (Vol. 5, p. 132).

2. Organized games are not the same as play.

"We do not say a word against the educational value of games. We know that many things are learned in the playing-fields; . . . But organised games are not *play* in the sense we have in view. Boys and girls must have time to invent episodes, carry on adventures, live heroic lives, lay sieges and carry forts, even if the fortress be an old armchair; and in these affairs the elders must neither meddle nor make" (Vol. 3, pp. 36, 37).

3. Be sensitive to interrupting a child's imaginative free play.

"They [the parents] must be content to know that they do not understand, and, what is more, that they carry with them a chill breath of reality which sweeps away

---

Notes

"There is a little danger in these days of much educational effort that children's play should be crowded out, or, what is from our present point of view the same thing, should be prescribed for and arranged until there is no more freedom of choice about play than that about work."

illusions. Think what it must mean to a general in command of his forces to be told by some intruder into the play-world to tie his shoe-strings!" (Vol. 3, p. 37).

4. Do not feel obligated to always play with your child.

"There is an idea afloat that children require to be taught to play—to play at being little fishes and lambs and butterflies. No doubt they enjoy these games which are made for them, but there is a serious danger. In this matter the child who goes too much on crutches never learns to walk; he who is most played with by his elders has little power of inventing plays for himself" (Vol. 3, p. 37).

Questions to Ask about Play

- Am I giving my child lots of time for free play?
- Do I understand the difference between organized games and play?
- Am I trying to be sensitive to interrupting my child's imaginative free play?
- Do I not feel obligated to always play with my child?

More Quotes on Play

"The most effective kind of education is that a child should play amongst lovely things."—Plato

"We don't stop playing because we grow old; we grow old because we stop playing."—George Bernard Shaw

---

"He who is most played with by his elders has little power of inventing plays for himself."

Chapter 8
Books & Stories

"What are you doing, honey?" Joe asked his wife. She was deep in thought at the kitchen table, making some sort of list next to her laptop.

"Tomorrow is library day," she replied distractedly.

"Okay. So . . . ," Joe said, sitting down across from her at the table and trying to catch her gaze.

Heather set down her pen. "I'm sorry, what did you ask?"

"I was wondering why a trip to the library tomorrow required so much concentration tonight," Joe asked with a smile.

Heather returned his smile. "Well, I want to make sure the children get good books. I have some recommendations and suggestions from other moms, so I'm checking which of those books are available at our library."

"I'm glad you don't let the kids grab any books they see. But why don't you just put these books on hold?" asked Joe. "It would save you the time of tracking each one down on the shelves."

"Yes, I know," replied Heather. "And I do that sometimes. But I also want the children to understand how a library is put together and how to find books in it. So when we have a little extra time, I put together a list of good books that we will probably find, and I help them locate and pull the books themselves."

Heather returned to her laptop, and Joe smiled again. "You know what?" he asked.

"What?" Heather glanced back up.

"I like the way you think," he said.

Charlotte's Thoughts on Books & Stories

1. Give your child the best books, not twaddle.

"At the same time, the child's capacity for knowledge is very limited; his mind is, in this respect at least, but a little phial with a narrow neck; and, therefore, it behooves the parent or teacher to pour in only of the best" (Vol. 1, p. 175).

"Teachers, and even parents, who are careful enough about their children's diet, are so reckless as to the sort of mental aliment offered to them, that I am exceedingly anxious to secure consideration for this question, of the lessons and literature proper for the little people" (Vol. 1, pp. 176, 177).

"They must grow up upon the best. There must never be a period in their lives when they are allowed to read or listen to twaddle or reading-made-easy. There is never a time when they are unequal to worthy thoughts, well put; inspiring tales, well told. Let Blake's 'Songs of Innocence' represent their standard in poetry; De Foe and Stevenson, in prose; and we shall train a race of readers who will demand *literature*—that is, the fit and beautiful expression of inspiring ideas and pictures of life" (Vol. 2, p. 263).

Notes

"Twaddle" refers to books that underestimate a child's intelligence, that talk down to him in diluted words.

"They must grow up upon the best."

"Guard the nursery; let nothing in that has not the true literary flavour; let the children grow up on a few books read over and over, and let them have none, the reading of which does not cost an appreciable mental effort. This is no hardship. Activity, effort, whether of body or mind, is joyous to a child" (Vol. 5, p. 215).

"One more thing is of vital importance; children must have books, living books; the best are not too good for them; anything less than the best is not good enough; and if it is needful to exercise economy, let go everything that belongs to soft and luxurious living before letting go the duty of supplying the books, and the frequent changes of books, which are necessary for the constant stimulation of the child's intellectual life" (Vol. 2, p. 279).

2. If necessary, in order to protect your high standard, request that random books not be given as gifts to your child.

"Perhaps a printed form to the effect that gifts of books to the children will not be welcome in such and such a family, would greatly assist in this endeavour" (Vol. 2, p. 263).

3. Use books that will cultivate your child's taste for good literature and words fitly spoken.

"On the whole, the children who grow up amongst their elders and are not provided with what are called children's books at all, fare the better on what they are able to glean for themselves from the literature of grown-up people" (Vol. 1, p. 175).

"We wish the children to grow up to find joy and refreshment in the taste, the flavour of a *book*. We do not mean by a book any printed matter in a binding, but a work possessing certain literary qualities able to bring that sensible delight to the reader which belongs to a literary word fitly spoken. It is a sad fact that we are losing our joy in literary form. We are in such haste to be instructed by facts or titillated by theories, that we have no leisure to linger over the mere putting of a thought. But this is our error, for words are mighty both to delight and to inspire" (Vol. 2, pp. 262, 263).

"The mischief begins in the nursery. No sooner can a child read at all than hosts of friendly people show their interest in him by a present of a 'pretty book.' A 'pretty book' is not necessarily a picture-book, but one in which the page is nicely broken up in talk or short paragraphs. Pretty books for the schoolroom age follow those for the nursery, and, nursery and schoolroom outgrown, we are ready for 'Mudie's' lightest novels; the succession of 'pretty books' never fails us; we have no time for works of any intellectual fibre, and we have no more assimilating power than has the schoolgirl who feeds upon cheese-cakes" (Vol. 5, p. 214).

4. Use books that will cultivate your child's imagination.

"Stories, again, of the Christmas holidays, of George and Lucy, of the amusements, foibles, and virtues of children in their own condition of life, leave nothing to the imagination. The children know all about everything so well that it never occurs to them to play at the situations in any one of these tales, or even to

---

Notes

You can find a list of books that our children enjoyed during the early years at http://SimplyCharlotteMason.com/planning/eyguide/eyreadalouds/

Charles Mudie founded a lending library in England in the 1800s and stocked it with novels. His selections became, in a sense, the best-seller list for that era.

"We are in such haste to be instructed by facts or titillated by theories, that we have no leisure to linger over the mere putting of a thought."

read it twice over. But let them have tales of the imagination, scenes laid in other lands and other times, heroic adventures, hairbreadth escapes, delicious fairy tales in which they are never roughly pulled up by the impossible—even where all is impossible, and they know it, and yet believe" (Vol. 1, p. 152).

"Now imagination does not descend, full-grown, to take possession of an empty house; like every other power of the mind, it is the merest germ of a power to begin with, and grows by what it gets; and childhood, the age of faith, is the time for its nourishing" (Vol. 1, p. 153).

"The children should have the joy of living in far lands, in other persons, in other times—a delightful double existence; and this joy they will find, for the most part, in their story-books" (Vol. 1, p. 153).

5. Allow some funny books but not too much nonsense reading.

"Books of 'comicalities' cultivate no power but the sense of the incongruous; and though life is the more amusing for the possession of such a sense, when cultivated to excess it is apt to show itself in a flippant habit. *Diogenes and the Naughty Boys of Troy* is irresistible, but it is not the sort of thing the children will live over and over, and 'play at' by the hour, as we have all played at Robinson Crusoe finding the footprints. They must have 'funny books,' but do not give the children too much nonsense reading" (Vol. 1, p. 152).

6. Take opportunities to verify and research any author's statements.

"The notion that any contemporary authority is infallible may be steadily undermined from infancy onwards, though at some sacrifice of ease and glory to the parents. 'I don't know' must take the place of the vague wise-sounding answer, the random shot which children's pertinacious questionings too often provoke. And 'I don't know' should be followed by the effort to know, the research necessary to find out. Even then, the possibility of error in a 'printed book' must occasionally be faced. The results of this kind of training in the way of mental balance and repose are invaluable" (Vol. 2, pp. 43, 44).

7. Carefully prepare some good stories to tell your child without a book in hand.

"Every father and mother should have a *repertoire* of stories—a dozen will do, beautiful stories beautifully told; children cannot stand variations. 'You left out the rustle of the lady's gown, mother!' expresses reasonable irritation; the child cannot endure a suggestion that the story he lives in is no more than the 'baseless fabric of a vision' " (Vol. 5, p. 216).

- Stories without books allow more scope for the imagination and time to digest what was heard.

"Away with books, and 'reading to'—for the first five or six years of life. The endless succession of story-books, scenes, shifting like a panorama before the child's vision, is a mental and moral dissipation; he gets nothing to grow upon, or is allowed no leisure to digest what he gets. It is contrary to nature, too" (Vol. 5, p. 216).

A **repertoire** *is a list or supply.*

"They must have 'funny books,' but do not give the children too much nonsense reading."

Notes

Märchen *refers to German fairy tales.*

In this section Charlotte Mason reviewed a book by Felix Adler, pulling from his writings what she believed to be valuable and what she disagreed with. She quoted his views on fairy tales here. Of Adler, Charlotte wrote, "The work before us is one which should find a place on the educated parent's book-shelves, not perhaps to be swallowed whole as a 'complete guide,' but to be studied with careful attention and some freedom of choice as to which counsel of perfection is worthy to be acted upon, and which other counsel may be rejected as not fitting in with that scheme of educational thought which the parent has already made for himself" (Vol. 5, p. 102).

"Every father and mother should have a *repertoire* of stories."

- Stories that require preparation will cause the parent to be more careful in his selections.

" 'Tell us about the little boy who saved Haarlem!' How often do the children who know it ask for that most hero-making of all tales! And here is another advantage of the story told over the story read. Lightly come, lightly go, is the rule for the latter. But if you have to make a study of your story, if you mean to appropriate it as bread of life for your children, why, you select with the caution of the merchantman seeking goodly pearls" (Vol. 5, p. 216).

- Stories allow the parent to feed the child's mind directly, rather than be the middleman between the author and the child.

"Again, in the story read, the parent is no more than the middleman; but the story told is *food* as directly and deliberately given as milk from the mother's breast. Wise parents, whose children sit with big eyes pondering the oft-told tale, could tell us about this" (Vol. 5, p. 216).

- Remember that children will outgrow story-time.

"But it must be borne in mind that the story told is as milk to the child at the breast. By-and-by comes the time when children must read, must learn, and digest for themselves" (Vol. 5, pp. 216, 217).

8. If you wish to use fairy tales, consider these guidelines.

- Tell the story; do not give it to the child to read himself.

" 'My first counsel is, Tell the story. Do not give it to the child to read. The child, as it listens to the *Märchen*, looks up with wide-opened eyes to the face of the person who tells the story, and thrills responsive to the touch of the earlier life of the race, which thus falls upon its own.' That is, our author feels, and rightly so, that traditions should be orally delivered. This is well worth noting" (Vol. 2, p. 106).

- Keep in the moral as a part of the story.

"His second counsel is equally important 'Do not,' he says, 'take the moral plum out of the fairy-tale pudding, but let the child enjoy it as a whole. . . . Treat the moral element as an incident, emphasise it indeed, but incidentally. Pluck it as a wayside flower.' " (Vol. 2, p. 106).

- Eliminate offensive and objectionable elements.

"Mr. Felix Adler's third counsel is, to eliminate from the stories whatever is merely superstitious, merely a relic of ancient animism, and, again, whatever is objectionable on moral grounds. In this connection he discusses the vexed question of how far we should acquaint children with the existence of evil in the world.

" 'My own view,' he says, 'is that we should speak in the child's hearing only of those lesser forms of evil, physical or moral, with which it is already acquainted.' On this ground he would rule out all the cruel stepmother stories, the unnatural father stories, and so on; though probably most of us would make an exception in favour of Cinderella, and its charming German rendering *Aschenbrödel*. I am inclined to think, too, that fairy tales suffer in vigour and charm when they are prepared for the children; and that Wordsworth is right in considering that the very knowledge of evil conveyed in fairy tales under a certain glamour, is of use in saving children from painful and injurious shocks in real life" (Vol. 2, p. 107).

Questions to Ask about Books & Stories

- Am I being careful to give my child the best books, not twaddle?
- Do I need to request that random books not be given to my child as a present?
- Am I trying to use books that will cultivate my child's taste for good literature and words fitly spoken?
- Am I using books that will cultivate my child's imagination?
- Do I allow some funny books but not too much nonsense reading?
- Am I trying to take opportunities to verify and research any author's statements?
- Have I carefully prepared some good stories to tell my child without a book in hand?
- If I use fairy tales, am I trying to tell the tale with the moral embedded in the story and removing objectionable elements?

More Quotes on Books & Stories

"Poetry is the art of uniting pleasure with truth."—Samuel Johnson

"Read the best books first, or you may not have a chance to read them at all."—Henry David Thoreau

"There are many little ways to enlarge your child's world. Love of books is the best of all."—Jackie Kennedy

"Good books, like good friends, are few and chosen; the more select, the more enjoyable."—Louisa May Alcott

"The love of learning, the sequestered nooks,
And all the sweet serenity of books."—Henry Wadsworth Longfellow

"A love of books, of holding a book, turning its pages, looking at its pictures, and living its fascinating stories goes hand-in-hand with a love of learning."—Laura Bush

"By-and-by comes the time when children must read, must learn, and digest for themselves."

Chapter 9
Language

Mom's eyes twinkled across the lunch table as she announced, "At the conclusion of our mid-day sustenance, I think we should traverse the avenues to a natural place of recreation."

A smile spread across five-year-old Abigail's face. This was one of her favorite games. "Yes, I think we should," she said. "But what about . . . um . . . the . . . dozing period?" And Abigail glanced at little Esther.

"Oh, you mean the regularly occurring activity that usually follows on the heels of our mid-day sustenance?" Mom inquired.

"Yes, exactly," replied Abigail.

"I contemplated that very question," Mom said. "But I came to the conclusion that a moderate length of time in fresh oxygen may produce more benefits on this particular day."

Abigail laughed. "Sounds good to me!" She turned to her little sister. "Esther, do you want to go to the park after lunch?"

Charlotte's Thoughts about Language

1. Remember that your child will naturally learn to speak the language used around him during his childhood.

"He [M. Gouin] returned to France, after a ten months' absence, and found that his little nephew—whom he had left, a child of two and a half, not yet able to talk—had in the interval done what his uncle had signally failed to do. 'What!' I thought; 'this child and I have been working for the same time, each at a language. He, playing round his mother, running after flowers, butterflies and birds, without weariness, without apparent effort, without even being conscious of his work, is able to say all he thinks, express all he sees, understand all he hears; and when he began his work, his intelligence was yet a futurity, a glimmer, a hope. And I, versed in the sciences, versed in philosophy, armed with a powerful will, gifted with a powerful memory . . . . have arrived at nothing, or at practically nothing!' " (Vol. 1, p. 305).

2. Teach your child to pronounce words correctly.

"Drill the children in pure vowel sounds, in the enunciation of final consonants; do not let them speak of 'walkin' ' and 'talkin',' of a 'fi-ine da-ay,' 'ni-ice boy-oys' " (Vol. 1, p. 133).

3. Expand your child's vocabulary by using a variety of words in everyday conversations and encouraging him to use the fittest word for each situation.

" 'Come and see the puff-puff, dear.' 'Do you mean the *locomotive*, grandmamma?' As a matter of fact, the child of four and five has a wider, more exact vocabulary in everyday use than that employed by his elders and betters, and is constantly adding

> "The child of four and five has a wider, more exact vocabulary in everyday use than that employed by his elders and betters, and is constantly adding to this vocabulary with surprising quickness."

Language

Notes

Ergo *means therefore.*

An epithet is a descriptive word or phrase.

to this vocabulary with surprising quickness; *ergo*, to give a child of this class a vocabulary is no part of direct education. Again, we know that nothing escapes the keen scrutiny of the little people. It is not their perceptive powers we have to train, but the habit of methodical observation and accurate record" (Vol. 2, p. 226).

"We are in a bad way for epithets: there are hardly more than a dozen current amongst us; and of these one person has seldom more than one or two in everyday use. A cup of tea, a dress, a picture, a book, a person,—is 'nice,' 'perfect,' 'delicious,' 'delightful,' 'jolly,' according to the speaker; not at all according to the thing spoken of. Adverbs help a little; a thing may be 'nice,' 'how nice!' or 'too awfully nice!' but the help is rather in the way of force than of variety. J. finds all agreeable things 'too awfully nice!' while B. finds the same things only 'nice' As a rule, things and persons have each one distinctive quality; to see what that is in a flash, and to express it in the fittest word, is a proof of genius, or of the highest culture. 'That abysmal question, the condition of East London':—if one had not known that the speaker was a man of just perceptions and wide range of thought, intimately conversant with the questions of the day, that one phrase of a short conversation would have conveyed all that and more. The fitness of this use of 'abysmal' stamped the speaker. Little children often surprise and amuse their elders by the fitness and elegance of their phraseology. We have only to foster this power of theirs, to put good words in their way, to treat the perpetual use of 'jolly' or 'delicious' as rather idiotic, and we are not only fitting our children to shine in society, but doing something to conserve the treasures of the beautiful mother-tongue of our inheritance. It might be worthwhile to hunt up good strong Saxon epithets for everyday use from the writers of the sixteenth and seventeenth centuries. Milton alone affords a treasure-trove. In the hymn beginning,

'Let us with a gladsome mind,'

there are half-a-dozen adjectives used with original force; perhaps half-a-dozen *peculiar to that hymn*, in their use if not in their form. We cannot go about talking of the 'golden-tressed sun'; that is too good for us; but to get 'gladsome' into our common speech is worth an effort. 'Happy-making,' again, in the wonderful *Ode to Time*,—could we have a fitter word for our best occasions?" (Vol. 5, pp. 217, 218).

4. Do not require a child younger than six years old to narrate.

"Until he is six, let Bobbie narrate only when and what he has a mind to. He must not be called upon to *tell* anything. Is this the secret of the strange long talks we watch with amusement between creatures of two, and four, and five? Is it possible that they narrate while they are still inarticulate, and that the other inarticulate person takes it all in? They try us, poor dear elders, and we reply 'Yes,' 'Really!' 'Do you think so?' to the babble of whose meaning we have no comprehension. Be this as it may; of what goes on in the dim region of 'under two' we have no assurance. But wait till the little fellow has words and he will 'tell' without end to whomsoever will listen to the tale, but, for choice, to his own compeers" (Vol. 1, pp. 231, 232).

5. If desired, teach your young child to speak a foreign language or two.

"It is the duty of the nation to maintain relations of brotherly kindness with other nations; therefore it is the duty of every family, as an integral part of the

> "Until he is six, let Bobbie narrate only when and what he has a mind to. He must not be called upon to *tell* anything."

nation, to be able to hold brotherly speech with the families of other nations as opportunities arise; therefore to acquire the speech of neighbouring nations is not only to secure an inlet of knowledge and a means of culture, but is a duty of that higher morality (the morality of the family) which aims at universal brotherhood; therefore every family would do well to cultivate two languages besides the mother tongue, even in the nursery" (Vol. 2, p. 7).

"Having occasion to speak in public of three little children, all aged three, belonging to different families, where one parent was English, the other German, I said that these three children of my acquaintance could each say everything they had to say, express the whole range of their ideas, with equal ease and fluency in the two languages" (Vol. 1, p. 307).

What is more, he has learned a language, two languages, if he has had the opportunity, and the writer has known of three languages being mastered by a child of three, and one of them was Arabic; mastered, that is, so far that a child can say all that he needs to say in any one of the three—the sort of mastery most of us wish for when we are travelling in foreign countries" (Vol. 6, p. 35).

Questions to Ask about Language

- Do I remember that my child will naturally learn to speak the language used around him during his childhood?
- Am I trying to teach my child to pronounce words correctly?
- Am I expanding my child's vocabulary by using a variety of words in everyday conversations and encouraging him to use the fittest word for each situation?
- Am I careful not to require a child younger than six years old to narrate?
- If desired, am I teaching my child to speak a foreign language or two?

More Quotes on Language

" 'I wish life was not so short,' he thought. 'Languages take such a time, and so do all the things one wants to know about.' "—J. R. R. Tolkien

"The man who does not know other languages, unless he is a man of genius, necessarily has deficiencies in his ideas."—Victor Hugo

"Language is the dress of thought."—Samuel Johnson

"By words the mind is winged."—Aristophanes

"A word fitly spoken is like apples of gold in pictures of silver."—Proverbs 25:11

Notes

See also the comments on foreign language lessons in chapter 5, page 61.

"Little children often surprise and amuse their elders by the fitness and elegance of their phraseology. We have only to foster this power of theirs, to put good words in their way."

Chapter 10
Music & Art

"So what am I missing for the nursery?" Kendra asked. She and her husband were adopting two little boys, and they were as excited as they could be. Today Kendra and her friend Lori were making a final round at a local department store.

"A CD player," advised Lori. "And a few CDs of beautiful music."

"Wait a minute," laughed Kendra. "I can't stand those little tinkling-bell-high-pitched-baby-nonsense songs that I hear in the baby stores."

"Good!" Lori replied. "Don't play those. Get a variety of *beautiful* music—some that will soothe your boys and help them sleep peacefully, some for active play time, and some for background music at lunch occasionally.

"I like that idea. Will you help me pick out some CDs?" asked Kendra.

"Certainly, let's head over to the music department. Oh, wait!" Lori stopped in her tracks and pointed to a display. "That's a Van Gogh, and it's half price. Your boys will get hours of entertainment looking at this picture."

"It has the right colors for the nursery," agreed Kendra, adding the picture to the shopping cart. "And you're right, it is much more interesting than this nursery-rhyme stencil I grabbed."

Lori smiled. "Your boys are going to cultivate a wonderful taste for good music and good art, my dear."

Charlotte's Thoughts on Music & Art

1. Surround your child with good music and singing.

"It would be hard to say how much that passes for inherited musical taste and ability is the result of the constant hearing and producing of musical sounds, the *habit* of music, that the child of musical people grows up with" (Vol. 1, p. 133).

"It has been proved that only three per cent of children are what is called 'tone-deaf'; and if they are taken at an early age it is astonishing how children who appear to be without ear, develop it and are able to enjoy listening to music with understanding" (Vol. 6, p. 218).

2. Remember that music appreciation does not necessarily require piano lessons.

"Musical Appreciation, of course, has nothing to do with playing the piano. It used to be thought that 'learning music' must mean this, and it was supposed that children who had no talent for playing were unmusical and would not like concerts. But Musical Appreciation had no more to do with playing an instrument than acting had to do with an appreciation of Shakespeare, or painting with enjoyment of pictures" (Vol. 6, p. 218).

Notes

Vulgar means "lacking refinement, culture, or taste."

Pseudo means false.

3. Do not allow vulgar or false art in your house, whether in a picture, book, or toy.

"Nothing vulgar in the way of print, picture-book, or toy should be admitted—nothing to vitiate a child's taste or introduce a strain of commonness into his nature" (Vol. 1, p. 131).

"In the first place, we shall permit no *pseudo* Art to be in the same house with our children; next, we shall bring our own facile tastes and opinions to some such searching test as we have indicated, knowing that the children imbibe the thoughts that are in us, whether we will or no" (Vol. 2, p. 262).

4. Even one or two reproductions of good art (however inexpensive they may be) can influence your child's tastes.

"It would be hard to estimate the refining, elevating influence of one or two well-chosen works of art, in however cheap a reproduction" (Vol. 1, p. 131).

5. Inspire your child with great ideas that recognize and appreciate good music and art.

"We shall inspire our children with those great ideas which shall create a demand, anyway, for great Art" (Vol. 2, p. 262).

Questions to Ask about Music & Art

- Am I surrounding my child with good music and singing?
- Do I realize that music appreciation does not necessarily require piano lessons?
- Am I trying to be watchful not to allow vulgar or fake art in my house, whether in a picture, book, or toy?
- Do I have on display one or two reproductions of good art (however inexpensive they may be)?
- Am I seeking to inspire my child with ideas that recognize and appreciate good music and art?

More Quotes on Music & Art

"Love of beauty is taste. The creation of beauty is art."—Ralph Waldo Emerson

"Beautiful music is the art of the prophets that can calm the agitations of the soul; it is one of the most magnificent and delightful presents God has given us."—Martin Luther

"Take a music bath once or twice a week for a few seasons, and you will find that it is to the soul what the water bath is to the body."—Oliver Wendell Holmes

"The best, most beautiful, and most perfect way that we have of expressing a sweet concord of mind to each other is by music."—Jonathan Edwards

"It would be hard to estimate the refining, elevating influence of one or two well-chosen works of art."

"Next to the Word of God, the noble art of music is the greatest treasure in the world."—Martin Luther

"Pictures deface walls more often than they decorate them."—William Wordsworth

"Every artist dips his brush in his own soul, and paints his own nature into his pictures."—Henry Ward Beecher

"In art, the hand can never execute anything higher than the heart can imagine."—Ralph Waldo Emerson

Notes

"We shall inspire our children with those great ideas which shall create a demand, anyway, for great Art."

Chapter 11
Spiritual Life

My dear Cari,

First I want you to know that I love you and pray for you every day. It has been such a privilege to watch you blossom from girlhood to womanhood and now motherhood.

I'm sure you will find many more opportunities to teach your child about God, but since you asked me to, I am writing down the things that I tried to do when you were small.

- I tried to keep my walk with the Lord alive and vibrant, and keep you close enough beside me that you would notice.
- When you were a newborn and needed to be rocked or walked in the wee hours of the night, I sang the name of Jesus to you in a simple little song until you fell back asleep.
- Daddy and I prayed over your crib, and when you were old enough to understand what bedtime was, we prayed with you at bedtime. And we tried to make sure we thanked God for you or for something you had learned that day.
- I read Bible stories to you.
- We prayed for friends and loved ones every morning after breakfast (Remember our Prayer Photo Album?), and anytime during the day when we heard news about one of them.
- We thanked God for the flowers, grass, trees, dogs, whatever you noticed on our walks. Those prayers were nothing long or elaborate, just "Thank You, God, for flowers."
- I tried to answer your Why questions with Biblical principles whenever I could. This one was a challenge ofttimes, because you could come up with some difficult questions. I remember you raised your voice to your sister, one time, and I told you to please try again with a kind voice. Of course, you asked Why, and I replied that God wants us to be kind. Well, when you asked Why God wants us to be kind, I had to think for a moment. The best I could do was "God is love, and we show His love when we are kind." I'm not sure you were satisfied, but you didn't ask that particular Why again.
- We often played CDs of psalms, hymns, and spiritual songs for you at nap times and bedtimes.
- And most importantly, but you probably never knew, we prayed for you constantly. We asked the Lord for wisdom to teach you His way and to nurture your personal relationship with Him.

Now we will have the privilege of expanding that prayer to ask the Lord to give

---

Notes

To learn more about a Prayer Photo Album, visit http://intentionalparents.com/2009/08/16/prayer-photo-album/

"God does love and cherish the little children all day long."

Spiritual Life

Notes

you wisdom as you teach your little one His way and seek to nurture him (or her, Do we know yet?) in the Lord. Hold tightly to God's hand, my dear; He is faithful, and He will gently lead you every step of the way.

Love,
Mom

Charlotte's Thoughts on Spiritual Life

1. Realize that it is your highest duty to nourish your child's spiritual life and point him toward God.

"It does not rest with the parent to choose whether he will or will not attempt to quicken and nourish this divine life in his child. To do so is his bounden duty and service. If he neglect or fail in this, I am not sure how much it matters that he has fulfilled his duties in the physical, moral and mental culture of his child, except in so far as the child is the fitter for the divine service should the divine life be awakened in him" (Vol. 1, pp. 343, 344).

"The parent must not make blundering, witless efforts: as this is the highest duty imposed upon him, it is also the most delicate; and he will have infinite need of faith and prayer, tact and discretion, humility, gentleness, love, and sound judgment, if he would present his child to God, and the thought of God to the soul of his child" (Vol. 1, p. 345).

2. Be careful to accurately represent God and the things of God to your child.

"Now listen to what goes on in many a nursery:—'God does not love you, you naughty, wicked boy!' 'He will send you to the bad, wicked place,' and so on; and this is all the practical teaching about the ways of his 'almighty Lover' that the child gets!—never a word of how God does love and cherish the little children all day long, and fill their hours with delight. Add to this, listless perfunctory prayers, idle discussions of Divine things in their presence, light use of holy words, few signs whereby the child can read that the things of God are more to his parents than any things of the world, and the child is hindered, tacitly forbidden to 'come unto Me,'—and this, often, by parents who in the depths of their hearts desire nothing in comparison with God" (Vol. 1, p. 20).

"Do not parents deliberately present God as an exactor, to back up the feebleness of their own government; and do they not freely utter, on the part of God, threats they would be unwilling to utter on their own part? Again, what child has not heard from his nurse this, delivered with much energy, 'God does not love you, you naughty boy! He will send you to the bad place!' And these two thoughts of God, as an exactor and a punisher, make up, often enough, all the idea the poor child gets of his Father in heaven. What fruit can come of this but aversion, the turning away of the child from the face of his Father? What if, instead, were given to him the thought well expressed in the words, 'The all-forgiving gentleness of God'?" (Vol. 1, p. 345).

"These are but two of many deterrent thoughts of God commonly presented to the tender soul; and the mother, who realises that the heart of her child may be

> "He will have infinite need of faith and prayer, tact and discretion, humility, gentleness, love, and sound judgment, if he would present his child to God, and the thought of God to the soul of his child."

irrevocably turned against God by the ideas of Him imbibed in the nursery, will feel the necessity for grave and careful thought, and definite resolve, as to what teaching her child shall receive on this momentous subject" (Vol. 1, p. 346).

"Faith is, then, the simple trust of person in Person. We realise with fearful joy that He is about our path, and about our bed, and spieth out all our ways—not with the austere eye of a judge, but with the caressing, if critical, glance of a parent" (Vol. 2, p. 135).

"It is a very sad fact that many children get their first ideas of God in the nursery, and that these are of a Being on the watch for their transgressions and always ready to chastise. It is hard to estimate the alienation which these first ideas of the divine Father set up in the hearts of His little children" (Vol. 3, p. 145).

"But what can the parent do? Just this, and no more: he can present the idea of God to the soul of the child" (Vol. 1, p. 344).

"It is his part to deposit, so to speak, within reach of the soul of the child some fruitful idea of God; the immature soul makes no effort towards that idea, but the living Word reaches down, touches the soul,—and there is *life*; growth and beauty, flower and fruit" (Vol. 1, p. 344).

3. Realize that your everyday conversation and attitudes can teach your child much about God.

"We see how the destiny of a life is shaped in the nursery, by the reverent naming of the Divine Name; by the light scoff at holy things; by the thought of duty the little child gets who is made to finish conscientiously his little task; by the hardness of heart that comes to the child who hears the faults or sorrows of others spoken of lightly" (Vol. 2, pp. 39, 40).

4. Carefully consider which ideas about God will minister most to your child and the best way to convey those ideas.

"Parents who recognise that their great work is to be done by the instrumentality of the ideas they are able to introduce into the minds of their children, will take anxious thought as to those ideas of God which are most fitting for children, and as to how those ideas may best be conveyed" (Vol. 2, p. 51).

"It is better that children should receive a few vital ideas that their souls may grow upon than a great deal of indefinite teaching" (Vol. 1, p. 346).

"How to select these few quickening thoughts of the infinite God? The selection is not so difficult to make as would appear at first sight. In the first place, we must teach that which we know, know by the life of the soul, not with any mere knowledge of the mind. Now, of the vast mass of the doctrines and the precepts of religion, we shall find that there are only a few vital truths that we have so taken into our being that we live upon them—this person, these; that person, those; some of us, not more than a single one. One or more, these are the truths we must teach the children, because these will come straight out of our hearts with the

"We must teach that which we know, know by the life of the soul, not with any mere knowledge of the mind."

Spiritual Life

Notes

enthusiasm of conviction which rarely fails to carry its own idea into the spiritual life of another" (Vol. 1, p. 346).

"The most important part of our subject remains to be considered—the inspiring ideas we propose to give children in the things of the divine life. This is a matter we are a little apt to leave to chance; but when we consider the vitalising power of an idea, and how a single great idea changes the current of a life, it becomes us to consider very carefully what ideas of the things of God we may most fitly offer children, and how these may be most invitingly presented" (Vol. 3, pp. 144, 145).

5. Look for teachable moments in everyday life to build up your child's faith with a few words.

"The next considerations that will press upon the mother are of the times, and the manner, of this teaching in the things of God. It is better that these teachings be rare and precious, than too frequent and slighty valued; better not at all, than that the child should be surfeited with the mere sight of spiritual food, rudely served" (Vol. 1, pp. 347, 348).

"At the same time, he must be built up in the faith, and his lessons must be regular and progressive; and here everything depends upon the tact of the mother. Spiritual teaching, like the wafted odour of flowers, should depend on which way the wind blows. Every now and then there occurs a holy moment, felt to be holy by mother and child, when the two are together—that is the moment for some deeply felt and softly spoken word about God, such as the occasion gives rise to. Few words need be said, no exhortation at all; just the flash of conviction from the soul of the mother to the soul of the child" (Vol. 1, p. 348).

"This is all: no routine of spiritual teaching; a dread of many words, which are apt to smother the fire of the sacred life; much self-restraint shown in the allowing of seeming opportunities to pass; and all the time, earnest purpose of heart, and a definite scheme for the building up of the child in the faith. It need not be added that, to make another use of our Lord's words, 'this kind cometh forth only by prayer.' It is as the mother gets wisdom liberally from above, that she will be enabled for this divine task" (Vol. 1, p. 348).

6. Present Christ as the Joy-giver.

"There are some ideas of the spiritual life more proper than others to the life and needs of the child. Thus, Christ the Joy-giver is more to him than Christ the Consoler" (Vol. 1, p. 347).

7. Present God as a loving and ever-present help to your child.

"Not a far-off God, a cold abstraction, but a warm, breathing, spiritual Presence about his path and about his bed—a Presence in which he recognises protection and tenderness in darkness and danger, towards which he rushes as the timid child to hide his face in his mother's skirts" (Vol. 2, p. 47).

"The Indwelling of Christ is a thought particularly fit for the children, because their large faith does not stumble at the mystery, their imagination leaps readily to

> "It becomes us to consider very carefully what ideas of the things of God we may most fitly offer children, and how these may be most invitingly presented."

the marvel, that the King Himself should inhabit a little child's heart" (Vol. 1, p. 352).

" 'Thou art about my path and about my bed and spiest out all my ways,' should be a thought, not of fear, but of very great comfort to every child. This constant recognition of authority excites the twofold response of docility and of reverence" (Vol. 3, p. 138).

8. Present God as Father and Giver to your child.

" 'Our Father, who is in heaven,' is perhaps the first idea of God which the mother will present to her child—Father and Giver, straight from whom comes all the gladness of every day. 'What a happy birthday our Father has given to my little boy!' 'The flowers are coming again; our Father has taken care of the life of the plants all through the winter cold!' 'Listen to that skylark! It is a wonder how our Father can put so much joy into the heart of one little bird.' 'Thank God for making my little girl so happy and merry!' Out of this thought comes prayer, the free utterance of the child's heart, more often in thanks for the little joys of the day counted up than in desire, just yet. The words do not matter; any simple form the child can understand will do; the rising Godward of the child-heart is the true prayer" (Vol. 1, pp. 349, 350).

"A child's whole notion of religion is 'being good.' It is well that he should know that being good is not his whole duty to God, although it is so much of it; that the relationship of love and personal service, which he owes as a child to his Father, as a subject to his King, is even more than the 'being good' which gives our Almighty Father such pleasure in His children" (Vol. 3, p. 136).

"Perhaps the first vitalising idea to give children is that of the tender Fatherhood of God; that they live and move and have their being within the divine embrace. Let children grow up in this joyful assurance, and, in the days to come, infidelity to this closest of all relationships will be as shameful a thing in their eyes as it was in the eyes of the Christian Church during the age of faith" (Vol. 3, p. 145).

9. Present God as King to your child.

"Let them grow up, too, with the shout of a King in their midst. There are, in this poor stuff we call human nature, founts of loyalty, worship, passionate devotion, glad service, which have, alas! to be unsealed in the earth-laden older heart, but only ask place to flow from the child's. There is no safeguard and no joy like that of being under orders, being possessed, controlled, continually in the service of One whom it is gladness to obey" (Vol. 2, p. 57).

"Next, perhaps, the idea of Christ their King is fitted to touch springs of conduct and to rouse the enthusiasm of loyalty in children, who have it in them, as we all know, to bestow heroic devotion on that which they find heroic" (Vol. 3, p. 145).

"Perhaps we do not make enough of this principle of hero-worship in human nature in our teaching of religion. We are inclined to make our religious aims subjective rather than objective. We are tempted to look upon Christianity as a

Spiritual Life

Notes

'scheme of salvation' designed and carried out for our benefit; whereas the very essence of Christianity is passionate devotion to an altogether adorable Person" (Vol. 3, p. 145).

10. Help your child understand that we are on earth to fight for the cause of Christ.

"We lose sight of the fact in our modern civilisation, but a king, a leader, implies warfare, a foe, victory—possible defeat and disgrace. And this is the conception of life which cannot too soon be brought before children.

" 'After thinking the matter over with some care, I resolved that I cannot do better than give you my view of what it was that the average boy carried away from our Rugby of half a century ago which stood him in the best stead—was of the highest value to him—in after life. . . . I have been in some doubt as to what to put first, and am by no means sure that the few who are left of my old schoolfellows would agree with me; but, speaking for myself, I think this was our most marked characteristic, the feeling that in school and close we were in training for a big fight—were, in fact, already engaged in it—a fight which would last all our lives, and try all our powers, physical, intellectual, and moral, to the utmost. I need not say that this fight was the world-old one of good with evil, of light and truth against darkness and sin, of Christ against the devil.'

"So said the author of *Tom Brown* in an address to Rugby School delivered on a recent Quinquagesima Sunday. This is plain speaking; education is only worthy of the name as it teaches this lesson; and it is a lesson which should be learnt in the home or ever the child sets foot in any other school of life. It is an insult to children to say they are too young to understand this for which we are sent into the world" (Vol. 2, pp. 57, 58).

Quinquagesima Sunday is the last Sunday before Lent.

11. Present Christ as the Savior and Forgiver of sins.

"But, recognising this, there is still a danger in these days of adopting a rose-water treatment in our dealings with children. Few grown-up people, alas! have so keen and vivid a sense of sin as a little transgressor say of six or seven. Many a naughty, passionate, or sulky and generally hardened little offender is so, simply because he does not know, with any personal knowledge, that there is a Saviour of the world, who has for him instant forgiveness and waiting love. But here again, the thoughts of a child should be turned outwards to Jesus, our Saviour, and not inward to his own thoughts and feelings towards our blessed Saviour" (Vol. 3, p. 146).

"A boy of five, a great-grandson of Dr Arnold, was sitting at the piano with his mother, choosing his Sunday hymn; he chose 'Thy will be done,' and, as his special favourite, the verse beginning 'Renew my will from day to day.' The choice of hymn and verse rather puzzled his mother, who had a further glimpse into the world of child-thought when the little fellow said wistfully, 'Oh, dear, it's very hard to do God's work!' The difference between doing and bearing was not plain to him, but the battle and struggle and strain of life already pressed on the spirit of the 'careless, happy child.' That an evil spiritual personality can get at their thoughts, and incite them to 'be naughty,' children learn all too soon and understand, perhaps, better than we do. Then, they are cross, 'naughty,' separate, sinful, needing to be healed as

"The thoughts of a child should be turned outwards to Jesus, our Saviour."

truly as the hoary sinner, and much more aware of their need, because the tender soul of the child, like an infant's skin, is fretted by spiritual soreness. 'It's very good of God to forgive me so often; I've been naughty so many times to-day,' said a sad little sinner of six, not at all because any one else had been at the pains to convince her of naughtiness. . . . We must needs smile at the little 'crimes,' but we must not smile too much, and let children be depressed with much 'naughtiness' when they should live in the instant healing, in the dear Name, of the Saviour of the world" (Vol. 2, pp. 58, 59).

12. Point out God's handiwork in creation.

"A mother knows how to speak of God as she would of an absent father with all the evidences of his care and love about her and his children. She knows how to make a child's heart beat high in joy and thankfulness as she thrills him with the thought, 'my Father made them all,' while his eye delights in flowery meadow, great tree, flowing river" (Vol. 6, p. 159).

13. Be careful to give your child a balance between duty to God our Creator and sentiment toward our Heavenly Father.

"Out of this thought, too, comes duty—the glad acknowledgement of the debt of service and obedience to a Parent so gracious and benign—not One who exacts service at the sword's point, as it were, but One whom His children run to obey" (Vol. 1, p. 350).

"The Christian parent will assuredly present the thought of Law in connection with a Law-giver, and will supplement the thousand valuable suggestions he will find here with his own strong conviction that 'Ought' is of the Lord God" (Vol. 2, p. 115).

"The idea of *duty* is not wrought into the very texture of their souls; and *duty* to Him who is invisible, which should be the very foundation of life, is least taught of all. I do not say that children are allowed to grow up without religious sentiments and religious emotions, and that they do not say quaint and surprising things, showing that they have an insight of their own into the higher life.

"But duty and sentiment are two things. Sentiment is optional; and young people grow up to think that they *may* believe in God, *may* fear God, *may* love God in a measure—but that they *must* do these things, that there is no choice at all about the love and service of God, that it is their duty, that which they *owe*, to love Him 'with all their heart, with all their mind, with all their soul, with all their strength,' these things are seldom taught and understood as they should be. Even where our sentiment is warm, our religious notions are lax; and children, the children of good, religious parents, grow up without that intimate, ever-open, ever-cordial, ever-corresponding relation with Almighty God, which is the very fulfilment of life" (Vol. 3, pp. 89, 90).

"But if children are brought up from the first with this magnet—'Ye are *not* your own'; the divine Author of your being has given you life, and a body finely adapted for His service; He gives you the work of preserving this body in health, nourishing it in strength, and training it in fitness for whatever special work He may give you

---

Notes

"That intimate, ever-open, ever-cordial, ever-corresponding relation with Almighty God, which is the very fulfilment of life."

to do in His world,—why, young people themselves would readily embrace a more Spartan regimen; they would desire to be available, and physical transgressions and excesses, however innocent they seem, would be self-condemned by the person who felt that he was trifling with a trust" (Vol. 3, p. 103).

"It is in their early years at home that children should be taught to realise that duty can exist only as that which we *owe* to God; that the law of God is exceeding broad and encompasses us as the air we breathe, only more so, for it reaches to our secret thoughts; and this is not a hardship but a delight" (Vol. 3, p. 128).

14. As soon as your child begins to speak, teach him to pray.

"Let us consider what is commonly done in the nursery in this respect. No sooner can the little being lisp than he is taught to kneel up in his mother's lap, and say 'God bless . . . .' and then follows a list of the near and dear, and 'God bless . . . . and make him a good boy, for Jesus' sake. Amen.' It is very touching and beautiful. I once peeped in at an open cottage door in a moorland village, and saw a little child in its nightgown kneeling in its mother's lap and saying its evening prayer. The spot has ever since remained to me a sort of shrine. There is no sight more touching and tender. By-and-by, so soon as he can speak the words,
    'Gentle Jesus, meek and mild,'
is added to the little one's prayer, and later, 'Our Father.' Nothing could be more suitable and more beautiful than these morning and evening approaches to God, the little children brought to Him by their mothers. And most of us can 'think back' to the hallowing influence of these early prayers" (Vol. 2, pp. 54, 55).

15. Let your child know that you pray for him.

"But might not more be done? How many times a day does a mother lift up her heart to God as she goes in and out amongst her children, and they never know! 'To-day I talked to them' (a boy and girl of four and five) 'about Rebekah at the well. They were very much interested, especially about Eliezer praying in his heart and the answer coming at once. They said, "How did he pray?" I said, "I often pray in my heart when you know nothing about it. Sometimes you begin to show a naughty spirit, and I pray for you in my heart, and almost directly I find the good spirit comes, and your faces show my prayer is answered." O. stroked my hand and said, "Dear mother, I shall think of that!" Boy looked thoughtful, but didn't speak; but when they were in bed I knelt down to pray for them before leaving them, and when I got up, Boy said, "Mother, God filled my heart with goodness while you prayed for us; and, mother, I *will* try to-morrow" ' " (Vol. 2, p. 55).

16. Share your spontaneous prayers before your child too.

"Is it possible that the mother could, when alone with her children, occasionally hold this communing out loud, so that the children might grow up in the sense of the presence of God? It would probably be difficult for many mothers to break down the barrier of spiritual reserve in the presence of even their own children. But, could it be done, would it not lead to glad and natural living in the recognised presence of God?" (Vol. 2, p. 55).

17. Let your child hear you thanking God for His goodness.

"A mother, who remembered a little penny scent-bottle as an early joy of her own, took three such small bottles home to her three little girls. They got them next morning at the family breakfast, and enjoyed them all through the meal. Before it ended the mother was called away, and little M. was sitting rather solitary with her scent-bottle and the remains of her breakfast. And out of the pure well of the little girl's heart came this, intended for nobody's ear, 'Dear mother, you are *too* good!' Think of the joy of the mother who should overhear her little child murmuring over the first primrose of the year, 'Dear God, you are *too* good!' Children are so imitative, that if they hear their parents speak out continually their joys and fears, their thanks and wishes, they, too, will have many things to say" (Vol. 2, pp. 55, 56).

18. Be careful that archaic language doesn't hinder your child from understanding and loving the things of God.

"But the little English child is thrust out in the cold by an archaic mode of address, reverent in the ears of us older people, but forbidding, we may be sure, to the child. Then, for the Lord's Prayer, what a boon would be a truly reverent translation of it into the English of to-day! To us, who have learned to spell it out, the present form is dear, almost sacred; but we must not forget that it is after all only a translation, and is, perhaps, the most archaic piece of English in modern use: 'which art,' commonly rendered 'chart,' means nothing for a child. 'Hallowed' is the speech of a strange tongue to him—not much more to us; 'trespasses' is a semi-legal term, never likely to come into his every-day talk; and no explanation will make 'Thy' have the same force for him as 'your.' To make a child utter his prayers in a strange speech is to put up a barrier between him and his 'Almighty Lover.' Again, might we not venture to teach our children to say 'Dear God'? A parent, surely, can believe that no austerely reverential style can be so sweet in the Divine Father's ears as the appeal to 'dear God' for sympathy in joy and help in trouble, which flows naturally from the little child who is 'used to God.' Let children grow up aware of the constant, immediate, joy-giving, joy-taking Presence in the midst of them, and you may laugh at all assaults of 'infidelity,' which is foolishness to him who knows his God as—only far better than—he knows father or mother, wife or child" (Vol. 2, pp. 56, 57).

19. Teach the Bible to your child reverently, dutifully, and diligently.

"The mind of the little child is an open field, surely 'good ground,' where, morning by morning, the sower goes forth to sow, and the seed is the Word. All our teaching of children should be given reverently, with the humble sense that we are invited in this matter to co-operate with the Holy Spirit; but it should be given dutifully and diligently, with the awful sense that our co-operation would appear to be made a condition of the Divine action; that the Saviour of the world pleads with us to 'Suffer the little children to come unto Me,' as if we had the power to hinder, as we know that we have" (Vol. 2, p. 48).

"Believing that faith comes by hearing, and hearing by the word of God, that the man is established in the Christian faith according as the child has been instructed, the question of questions for us, is, how to secure that the children shall be well grounded in the Scriptures by their parents, and shall pursue the study with intelligence, reverence, and delight" (Vol. 2, p. 100).

"Another danger is, lest the things of the divine life should be made too familiar and hackneyed, that the name of our blessed Lord should be used without reverence; and that children should get the notion that the Lord God exists for their uses, and not they, for His service" (Vol. 3, p. 145).

20. Share Bible stories with your child from the time he is an infant.

"But let the imaginations of children be stored with the pictures, their minds nourished upon the words, of the gradually unfolding story of the Scriptures, and they will come to look out upon a wide horizon within which persons and events take shape in their due place and due proportion. By degrees, they will see that the world is a stage whereon the goodness of God is continually striving with the wilfulness of man; that some heroic men take sides with God; and that others, foolish and headstrong, oppose themselves to Him. The fire of enthusiasm will kindle in their breast, and the children, too, will take their side, without much exhortation, or any thought or talk of spiritual experience" (Vol. 1, p. 249).

"It is a matter of question when the child should first learn the 'Story of the Cross.' One thinks it would be very delightful to begin with Moses and the prophets: to go through the Old Testament history, tracing the gradual unfolding of the work and character of the Messiah; and then, when their minds are full of the expectation of the Jews, to bring before them the mystery of the Birth in Bethlehem, the humiliation of the Cross. But perhaps no gain in freshness of presentation would make up to the children for not having grown up with the associations of Calvary and Bethlehem always present to their minds" (Vol. 1, pp. 351, 352).

"We should not present Bible stories as carrying only the same moral sanction as the myths of ancient Greece; neither should we defer their introduction until the child has gone through a moral course of fairy tales and a moral course of fables. He should not be able to recall a time before the sweet stories of old filled his imagination; he should have heard the voice of the Lord God in the garden in the cool of the evening; should have been an awed spectator where the angels ascended and descended upon Jacob's stony pillow; should have followed Christ through the cornfield on the Sabbath-day, and sat in the rows of the hungry multitudes—so long ago that such sacred scenes form the unconscious background of his thoughts" (Vol. 2, pp. 108, 109).

21. Be careful to keep Bible story time fresh and delightful.

"Let the minds of young children be well stored with the beautiful narratives of the Old Testament and of the gospels; but, in order that these stories may be always fresh and delightful to them, care must be taken lest Bible teaching stale upon their minds" (Vol. 1, p. 251).

"Let all the circumstances of the daily Bible reading—the consecutive reading, from the first chapter of Genesis onwards, *with necessary omissions*—be delightful to the child; let him be in his mother's room, in his mother's arms; let that quarter of an hour be one of sweet leisure and sober gladness, the child's whole interest being allowed to go to the story without distracting moral considerations; and then, the less talk the better; the story will sink in, and bring its own teaching, a little now, and more every year as he is able to bear it. One such story will be in him a constantly growing, fructifying moral idea" (Vol. 1, p. 337).

"What is required of us is, that we should implant a *love* of the Word; that the most delightful moments of the child's day should be those in which his mother reads for him, with sweet sympathy and holy gladness in voice and eyes, the beautiful stories of the Bible; and now and then in the reading will occur one of those convictions, passing from the soul of the mother to the soul of the child, in which is the life of the Spirit" (Vol. 1, p. 349).

22. Select your Bible translation carefully when reading to your child, and be careful not to comment on every verse.

"It is a mistake to translate Bible stories into slipshod English, even when the narrator keeps close to the facts of the narrative. The rhythm and cadence of Biblical phraseology is as charming to a child as to his elders, if not more so. Read your Bible story to the child, bit by bit; get him to tell you in his own words (keeping as close as he can to the Bible words) what you have read, and then, if you like, talk about it; but not much. Above all, do not let us attempt a 'practical commentary on every verse in Genesis,' to quote the title of a work lately published" (Vol. 2, p. 110).

"We are apt to believe that children cannot be interested in the Bible unless its pages be watered down—turned into the slipshod English we prefer to offer them" (Vol. 1, pp. 247, 248).

"Read bit by bit (of the Old Testament anyway) to the children, as beautifully as may be, requiring them to tell the story, after listening, as nearly in the Bible words as they can" (Vol. 2, p. 112).

"A word about the reading of the Bible. I think we make a mistake in burying the text under our endless comments and applications. Also, I doubt if the picking out of individual verses, and grinding these into the child until they cease to have any meaning for him, is anything but a hindrance to the spiritual life. The Word is full of vital force, capable of applying itself" (Vol. 1, pp. 348, 349).

23. Omit or reword those portions of Bible accounts that would be inappropriate for young children.

"Let all the circumstances of the daily Bible reading—the consecutive reading, from the first chapter of Genesis onwards, *with necessary omissions*—be delightful to the child" (Vol. 1, p. 337).

"There are recitals in the Bible which we certainly should not put into the hands of children in any other book. We should do well to ask ourselves gravely, if we have any warrant for supposing that our children will be shielded from the suggestions

---

Notes

Remember that narration (telling in his own words) should not be required before the child is six years old. (See page 90.)

"What is required of us is, that we should implant a *love* of the Word."

of evil which we deliberately lay before them" (Vol. 2, p. 111).

24. Be careful of using Scripture to berate a child for his faults.

"Above all, do not read the Bible *at* the child: do not let any words of the Scriptures be occasions for gibbeting his faults. It is the office of the Holy Ghost to convince of sin; and He is able to use the Word for this purpose, without risk of that hardening of the heart in which our clumsy dealings too often result" (Vol. 1, p. 349).

25. Don't depend on the Sunday School to cultivate your child's spiritual life.

"That parents should make over the religious education of their children to a Sunday School is, no doubt, as indefensible as if they sent them for their meals to a table maintained by the public bounty" (Vol. 2, p. 92).

"Our Sunday Schools are used by those toil-worn and little-learned parents who are willing to accept at the hands of the more leisured classes this service of the religious teaching of their children. That is, the Sunday School is, at present, a necessary evil, an acknowledgment that there are parents so hard pressed that they are unable for their first duty" (Vol. 2, p. 92).

"Here we have the theory of the Sunday School—the parents who can, teach their children at home on Sunday, and substitutes step in to act for those who can not" (Vol. 2, pp. 92, 93).

26. Help your child cultivate the habit of thought of God.

"Of the child it should be said that God is in all his thoughts; happy-making, joyous thoughts, restful and dutiful thoughts, thoughts of loving and giving and serving, the wealth of beautiful thoughts with which every child's heart overflows" (Vol. 3, p. 140).

"We are inclined to think that a child is a little morbid and precocious when he asks questions and has imaginings about things divine, and we do our best to divert him. What he needs is to be guided into true, happy thinking; every day should bring him 'new thoughts of God, new hopes of heaven.' He understands things divine better than we do, because his ideas have not been shaped to a conventional standard; and thoughts of God are to him an escape into the infinite from the worrying limitations, the perception of the prison bars, which are among the bitter pangs of childhood" (Vol. 3, pp. 140, 141).

Questions to Ask about Spiritual Life

- Do I realize that it is my highest duty to nourish my child's spiritual life and point him toward God?
- Am I careful to accurately represent God and the things of God to my child?
- Am I remembering that my everyday conversation and attitudes can teach my child much about God?
- Am I carefully considering which ideas about God will minister most to my child and the best way to convey those ideas?

- Am I looking for teachable moments in everyday life to build up my child's faith with a few words?
- Do I present Christ as the Joy-giver?
- Do I present God as a loving and ever-present help?
- Do I present God as Father and Giver?
- Do I present God as King?
- Am I helping my child understand that we are on earth to fight for the cause of Christ?
- Do I present Christ as the Savior and Forgiver of sins?
- Am I trying to point out God's handiwork in creation?
- Am I being careful to give my child a balance between duty to God our Creator and sentiment toward our Heavenly Father?
- Am I teaching my child to pray?
- Do I let my child know that I am praying for him? (And am I faithful to pray for him?)
- Am I trying to share my spontaneous prayers before my child?
- Do I let my child hear me thanking God for His goodness?
- Am I being careful that archaic language doesn't hinder my child from understanding and loving the things of God?
- Am I trying to teach the Bible to my child reverently, dutifully, and diligently?
- Am I sharing Bible stories with my child from the time he is an infant?
- Am I doing all I can to keep Bible story time fresh and delightful?
- Have I selected the Bible translation carefully when reading to my child?
- Am I curbing my tendency to comment on every verse?
- Do I omit or reword those portions of Bible accounts that would be inappropriate for young children?
- Am I careful not to use Scripture to berate a child for his faults?
- Am I accepting personal responsibility rather than depending on the Sunday School to cultivate my child's spiritual life?
- Am I trying to help my child cultivate the habit of thought of God?

More Quotes on Spiritual Life

"The Bible is worth all the other books which have ever been printed."—Patrick Henry

"He prayeth best who loveth best
All things, both great and small."—Samuel Taylor Coleridge

"Let never day nor night unhallowed pass
But still remember what the Lord hath done."—William Shakespeare

"And thou shalt love the Lord thy God with all thine heart, and with all thy soul, and with all thy might. And these words, which I command thee this day, shall be in thine heart: And thou shalt teach them diligently unto thy children, and shalt talk of them when thou sittest in thine house, and when thou walkest by the way, and when thou liest down, and when thou risest up."—Deuteronomy 6:5–7

"Of the child it should be said that God is in all his thoughts."

Chapter 12
The Alphabet

Lunch was over as far as three-year-old Tina was concerned. *I don't want to make her wait in her chair until I'm done,* thought Heidi. *But if I let her go play, it will be hard to corral her for her nap.*

Heidi's gaze fell on the magnetic letters on the refrigerator. Quickly she cleared them all off except the *A* and the *B*.

Returning to her seat, she addressed her daughter. "Tina, bring me the letters from the refrigerator and I'll show you something."

While Heidi grabbed a bite of her sandwich, Tina eagerly picked the *A* and the *B* off the refrigerator and brought them over to the table.

"Thank you," said Heidi. She picked up the *B*. "This is a *B*," she stated simply. Then she laid it back on the table. "Can you find *B*?" she asked Tina.

Tina picked up the letter *B*.

"That's right," Heidi encouraged her. "You may put *B* on the refrigerator."

Tina did so while Heidi grabbed another bite of her sandwich.

Heidi picked up the *A* next. "This is *A*. Please put *A* on the refrigerator too."

After Tina had replaced both letters, Heidi asked, "Can you bring me *A*?" and took another bite of her sandwich.

Tina picked up the *A* and brought it to the table.

"Good job!" Heidi nodded. "Now can you get *B*?"

Two more bites and Heidi was done with her sandwich. *This worked pretty well,* she thought. *I'll add the C tomorrow.*

Charlotte's Thoughts on the Alphabet

1. Give your child letters that he can touch and handle—whether lettered wooden blocks, magnetic letters, or whatever—both upper case and lower case.

"As for his letters, the child usually teaches himself. He has his box of ivory letters and picks out *p* for pudding, *b* for blackbird, *h* for horse, big and little, and knows them both" (Vol. 1, p. 201).

2. Draw letters in the air and see if your child can name them, thus encouraging the habit of careful observation.

"But the learning of the alphabet should be made a means of cultivating the child's observation: he should be made to *see* what he looks at. Make big *B* in the air, and let him name it" (Vol. 1, p. 201).

3. Let your child draw letters in the air or in a tray of sand and you name them.

"Then let him make round *O*, and crooked *S*, and *T* for Tommy, and you name the letters as the little finger forms them with unsteady strokes in the air. To make

---

Notes

Let your child progress at his own pace in learning the alphabet. Please don't feel like these activities are requirements for your toddlers!

"The learning of the alphabet should be made a means of cultivating the child's observation: he should be made to *see* what he looks at."

The Alphabet

Notes

the small letters thus from memory is a work of more art, and requires more careful observation on the child's part. A tray of sand is useful at this stage. The child draws his finger boldly through the sand, and then puts a back to his *D*; and behold, his first essay in making a straight line and a curve" (Vol. 1, p. 201).

4. Be creative and use whatever you have to teach the alphabet.

"But the devices for making the learning of the 'A B C' interesting are endless" (Vol. 1, p. 201).

5. Do not hurry your child to learn all the A B C's.

"There is no occasion to hurry the child" (Vol. 1, p. 201).

6. Let your child find all the uppercase D*'s and lowercase* d*'s (or another letter he has learned) on a page of large print.*

"Let him learn one form at a time, and know it so well that he can pick out the *d*'s, say, big and little, in a page of large print" (Vol. 1, p. 201).

7. Teach your child the sounds that the letters make.

"Let him say *d* for duck, dog, doll, thus: *d*—uck, *d*—og, prolonging the sound of the initial consonant, and at last sounding *d* alone, not *dee*, but *d'*, the mere sound of the consonant separated as far as possible from the following vowel" (Vol. 1, p. 201).

8. Many children will learn the alphabet on their own, but there is no harm in teaching it when approached as play.

"Let the child alone, and he will learn the alphabet for himself: but few mothers can resist the pleasure of teaching it; and there is no reason why they should, for this kind of learning is no more than play to the child, and if the alphabet be *taught* to the little student, his appreciation of both form and sound will be cultivated" (Vol. 1, pp. 201, 202).

9. You can begin teaching the alphabet whenever the child shows an interest in his box of letters, as long as you keep it a game.

"When should he begin? Whenever his box of letters begins to interest him. The baby of two will often be able to name half a dozen letters; and there is nothing against it so long as the finding and naming of letters is a game to him" (Vol. 1, p. 202).

10. Be careful not to push, tease, or show off your child's progress in learning the alphabet.

"But he must not be urged, required to show off, teased to find letters when his heart is set on other play" (Vol. 1, p. 202).

Questions to Ask about The Alphabet

- Does my child have letters that he can touch and handle, both upper case and lower case?

> "Let the child alone, and he will learn the alphabet for himself: but few mothers can resist the pleasure of teaching it."

- Do I draw letters in the air and see if my child can name them?
- Do I encourage my child to draw letters in the air or in a tray of sand for me to name?
- Am I using whatever I have handy to teach the alphabet?
- Am I being careful not to hurry my child to learn all the A B C's?
- Do I give my child opportunities to find the letters he knows on a page of printed words in large type?
- Am I teaching my child the sounds that the letters make?
- Am I approaching these lessons as play for my child?
- Has my child shown an interest in his box of letters? If not, am I being careful not to push him into learning the alphabet?
- Am I trying not to push, tease, or show off my child's progress?

More Quotes about The Alphabet

"What we want is to see the child in pursuit of knowledge, and not knowledge in pursuit of the child."—George Bernard Shaw

"The man who can make hard things easy is the educator."—Ralph Waldo Emerson

"He must not be urged, required to show off, teased to find letters when his heart is set on other play."

Chapter 13
A Gifted Child

"Do you have a minute?" Sandy asked, approaching the swings and Evelyn eagerly. She had grown to respect this older mom's counsel, and she looked forward to the autumn park days that afforded regular opportunities to talk with her.

"Certainly, Sandy," replied Evelyn, pushing her youngest in the baby swing. "What's up?"

"Well, you know how Tommy has a great talent at drawing," Sandy began.

"Oh, yes," Evelyn agreed. "God has definitely given Tommy a gift."

Sandy smiled, then furrowed her brow. "I won't go into all the details, but a professor at the local art school wants to teach him." She went on hurriedly, "I'm sure it would be a wonderful opportunity to develop this talent even more, and he does love to draw, and it's not too far away, and it wouldn't cost us anything—she's willing to teach him for free because she's writing her thesis on gifted children and art. But I don't know what to do." Sandy looked at Evelyn expectantly.

Evelyn took her time forming her thoughts. "It does sound like an interesting opportunity," she said at last. "I guess I would have two questions for you to consider. First, does Tommy want to do it? And second, would it hinder Tommy's ability to be a typical little boy?"

Sandy nodded thoughtfully.

"In other words, be careful that you're not forcing Tommy to use his gift or develop his gift more fully. It needs to be his idea, something he wants to do," explained Evelyn. "And though Tommy is an artist, he is first and foremost a little boy. He needs lots of free time to play and explore. He needs a wide variety of interests and lots of exercise. He needs plenty of rest and fun, too. I don't know what all would be involved in this opportunity you've mentioned, but I believe those elements of Tommy's boyhood need to have first priority."

Evelyn chuckled then and pointed across the grass. Sandy followed her gaze and smiled too as she saw Tommy handing one of Evelyn's children a new sketch of ducks on the pond. "And whatever you decide," finished Evelyn, "make sure you keep encouraging him to share his gift with others. My Sammy loves those drawings!"

Charlotte's Thoughts on A Gifted Child

1. Nourish and cherish any special gifts you notice in your child.

"The duteous father and mother, on the contrary, who discern any lovely family trait in one of their children, set themselves to nourish and cherish it as a gardener the peaches he means to show" (Vol. 2, pp. 75, 76).

"The choicer the plant, the gardener tells us, the greater the pains must he take with the rearing of it: and here is the secret of the loss and waste of some of the most beauteous and lovable natures the world has seen; they have not had the pains

> "The choicer the plant, the gardener tells us, the greater the pains must he take with the rearing of it."

A Gifted Child

Notes

taken with their rearing that their delicate, sensitive organisations demanded" (Vol. 2, p. 76).

2. No matter in what area(s) your child is gifted, provide four things: exercise, nourishment, change, and rest.

"It is, at first sight, bewildering to perceive that for whatever distinctive quality, moral or intellectual, we discern in the children, special culture is demanded; but, after all, our obligation towards each such quality resolves itself into providing for it these four things: nourishment, exercise, change, and rest" (Vol. 2, p. 76).

3. Allow your child to exercise his special gifting; let him use it.

"A child has a great turn for languages (his grandfather was the master of nine); the little fellow 'lisps in Latin,' learns his *'mensa'* from his nurse, knows his declensions before he is five. What line is open to the mother who sees such an endowment in her child? First, let him use it; let him learn his declensions, and whatever else he takes to without the least sign of effort. Probably the Latin case-endings come as easily and pleasantly to his ear as does 'See-saw, Margery Daw,' to the ordinary child, though no doubt 'Margery Daw' is the wholesomer kind of thing" (Vol. 2, p. 76).

4. Be careful not to push him or put him on display.

"Let him do just so much as he takes to of his own accord; but never urge, never applaud, never show him off" (Vol. 2, p. 77).

5. Nourish your child's mind with ideas that relate to his gifting.

"It is a great thing that the child should get the *ideas* proper to the qualities inherent in him. An idea fitly put is taken in without effort, and, once in, ideas behave like living creatures—they feed, grow, and multiply" (Vol. 2, p. 77).

6. Provide delightful opportunities for a change of thought altogether different from his gifting, something like nature study or handicrafts.

"Next, provide him with some one delightful change of thought, that is, with work and ideas altogether apart from his bent for languages. Let him know, with friendly intimacy, the out-of-door objects that come in his way—the redstart, the rosechaffer, the ways of the caddis-worm, forest trees, field flowers—all natural objects, common and curious, near his home. No other knowledge is so delightful as this common acquaintance with natural objects.

"Or, again, some one remarks that all our great inventors have in their youth handled material—clay, wood, iron, brass, pigments. Let him work in material. To provide a child with delightful resources on lines opposed to his natural bent is the one way of keeping a quite sane mind in the presence of an absorbing pursuit" (Vol. 2, p. 77)

7. Also provide plenty of opportunities for fun and rest.

"At the same time, change of occupation is not rest: if a man ply a machine, now with his foot, and now with his hand, the foot or the hand rests, but the man does not. A game of romps (better, so far as mere rest goes, than games with laws

> "Let him do just so much as he takes to of his own accord; but never urge, never applaud, never show him off."

and competitions), nonsense talk, a fairy tale, or to lie on his back in the sunshine, should rest the child, and of such as these he should have his fill" (Vol. 2, p. 78).

"Another plea for abundant rest is that one thing at a time, and that done well, appears to be Nature's rule; and his hours of rest and play are the hours of the child's physical growth" (Vol. 2, p. 78).

8. Encourage your child to use his gifts to benefit others.

"It rests with parents to see that the dreariness of a motiveless life does not settle, sooner or later, on any one of their children" (Vol. 2, p. 81).

"The mother, to whom her child is as an open book, must find a vent for the restless workings of his nature, the more apt to be troubled by—
 'The burden of the mystery,
 The heavy and the weary weight
 Of all this unintelligible world'—
the more finely he is himself organised. Fill him with the enthusiasm of humanity. Whatever gifts he has, let them be cultivated as 'gifts for men.' 'The thing best worth living for is *to be of use*,' was well said lately by a thinker who has left us; and the child into whose notion of life that idea is fitted will not grow up to find time heavy on his hands. The life blessed with an enthusiasm will not be dull; but a weight must go into the opposite scale to balance even the noblest enthusiasm. As we have said, open for him some door of natural science, some way of mechanical skill; in a word, give the child an absorbing pursuit and a fascinating hobby, and you need not fear eccentric or unworthy developments" (Vol. 2, p. 81).

Questions to Ask about A Gifted Child

- Am I trying to nourish and cherish any special gifts I have noticed in my child?
- Am I allowing my child to exercise his special gifting?
- Am I being careful not to push him or put him on display?
- Am I trying to nourish my child's mind with ideas that relate to his gifting?
- Do I provide delightful opportunities for a change of thought altogether different from his gifting?
- Am I providing plenty of opportunities for fun and rest?
- Am I encouraging my child to use his gifts to benefit others?

More Quotes on A Gifted Child

"The greatest virtues are those which are most useful to other persons."—Aristotle

"I want to help you to grow as beautiful as God meant you to be when he thought of you first."—George MacDonald

"Whatever gifts he has, let them be cultivated as 'gifts for men.'"

Appendix

Charlotte's Thoughts on Kindergarten. 121
Beginning Reading 130
    Preparation for Reading. 131
    Reading Lessons Guidelines 133
    Two Mothers' Conversation 135
    Some Beginning Reading Lesson Plans 138
Math Concepts 141
Handwriting. 142

Charlotte's Thoughts on Kindergarten

1. The home ought to be the best growing-ground for little children.

"Whatever be the advantages of *Kindergarten* or other schools for little children, the home schoolroom ought to be the best growing-ground for them" (Vol. 1, p. 170).

2. The success of a Kindergarten class depends largely on the quality of the teacher.

"It is hardly necessary, here, to discuss the merits of the Kindergarten School. The success of such a school demands rare qualities in the teacher—high culture, some knowledge of psychology and of the art of education; intense sympathy with the children, much tact, much common sense, much common information, much 'joyousness of nature,' and much governing power;—in a word, the Kindergarten method is nicely contrived to bring the child *en rapport* with a superior intelligence. Given, such a superior being to conduct it, and the Kindergarten is beautiful—''tis like a little heaven below'; but put a commonplace woman in charge of such a school, and the charmingly devised gifts and games and occupations become so many instruments of *wooden* teaching" (Vol. 1, p. 178).

3. The mother is naturally qualified to be her child's best teacher.

"If the very essence of the Kindergarten method is personal influence, a sort of spiritual mesmerism, it follows that the mother is naturally the best *Kindergartnerin*; for who so likely as she to have the needful tact, sympathy, common sense, culture?" (Vol. 1, p. 178).

4. A mother can adapt and implement the principles of a good Kindergarten at home without having to adhere to its rigid practices.

"Though every mother should be a *Kindergartnerin*, in the sense in which Froebel would employ the term, it does not follow that every nursery should be a regularly organised Kindergarten. Indeed, the machinery of the Kindergarten is no more than a device to ensure the carrying out of certain educational *principles*, and some of these it is the mother's business to get at, and work out according to Froebel's method—or her own" (Vol. 1, p. 179).

"On the whole, we may say that some of the *principles* which should govern Kindergarten training are precisely those in which every thoughtful mother endeavours to bring up her family; while the *practices* of the Kindergarten, being only ways, amongst others, of carrying out these principles, and being apt to become stereotyped and wooden, are unnecessary, but may be adopted so far as they fit in conveniently with the mother's general scheme for the education of her family" (Vol. 1, p. 181).

Notes

A few years before Charlotte Mason was born, Friedrich Froebel started a Play and Activity Institute for young children in Germany. He called this institute "Kindergarten," which means "child's garden." The main activities of his kindergarten were singing, dancing, gardening, and self-directed play with Froebel Gifts. These Gifts were basic toys, such as building blocks or a ball on a string. Over the years, as Kindergartens were established in various countries, the simplicity and self-directed play that Froebel emphasized were replaced with more teacher-directed activities.

En rapport *means "in agreement."*

Appendix

Notes

Bona fide *means "in good faith" and refers to sincere and honest intentions.*

"There is always the danger that a method, a *bona fide* method, should degenerate into a mere system. The *Kindergarten Method*, for instance, deserves the name, as having been conceived and perfected by large-hearted educators to aid the many-sided evolution of the living, growing, most complex human being; but what a miserable wooden *system* does it become in the hands of ignorant practitioners!" (Vol. 1, pp. 8, 9).

5. While it is true that a child may learn good things at a Kindergarten, it is usually too narrow a focus and too prescribed a curriculum.

"For instance, in the Kindergarten the child's *senses* are carefully and progressively trained: he looks, listens, learns by touch; gets ideas of size, colour, form, number; is taught to copy faithfully, express exactly. And in this training of the senses, the child is made to pursue the method the infant shapes for himself in his early studies of ring or ball.

"But it is possible that the child's marvellous power of obtaining knowledge by means of his senses may be undervalued; that the field may be too circumscribed; and that, during the first six or seven years in which he might have become intimately acquainted with the properties and history of every natural object within his reach, he has obtained, *exact* ideas, it is true—can distinguish a rhomboid from a pentagon, a primary from a secondary colour, has learned to *see* so truly that he can copy what he sees in folded paper or woven straw,—but this at the expense of much of that *real knowledge* of the external world which at no time of his life will he be so fitted to acquire. Therefore, while the *exact* nicely graduated training of the Kindergarten may be of value, the mother will endeavour to give it by the way, and will by no means let it stand for that wider training of the senses, to secure which for her children is a primary duty" (Vol. 1, pp. 179, 180).

6. A child may be taught the habit of best effort at home through a thousand opportunities and without the anxiety that usually accompanies a classroom setting.

"Again, the child in the Kindergarten is set to such tasks only as he is competent to perform, and then, whatever he has to do, he is expected to do *perfectly*. I have seen a four-years-old child blush and look as self-condemend, because he had folded a slip of paper irregularly, as if found out in a falsehood. But mother or nurse is quite able to secure that the child's small offices are perfectly executed; and, here is an important point, without that slight strain of distressful anxiety which may be observed in children labouring to please that smiling goddess, their 'Kindergarnerin.'

Occupations in Froebel's Kindergarten were materials used to practice certain skills, somewhat akin to handicrafts.

"The Kindergarten 'Occupations' afford opportunities for training in this kind of faithfulness; but in the home a thousand such opportunities occur; if only in such trifles as the straightening of a tablecloth or of a picture, the hanging of a towel, the packing of a parcel—every thoughtful mother invents a thousand ways of training in her child a just eye and a faithful hand" (Vol. 1, p. 180).

7. Little games and activities can be used if they will help, but a mother can make use of all the natural activities of a typical day at home to further her child's education.

"Nevertheless, as a means of methodical training, as well as of happy employment, the introduction of some of the games and occupations of the Kindergarten into the nursery may be allowed; provided that the mother does not depend upon these, but makes *all* the child's occupations subserve the purposes of his education" (Vol. 1, p. 180).

8. An atmosphere of gentleness and serenity should be cultivated, whether in a school setting or at home.

"The child breathes an atmosphere of 'sweetness and light' in the Kindergarten. You see the sturdy urchin of five stiffen his back and decline to be a jumping frog, and the *Kindergartnerin* comes with unruffled gentleness, takes him by the hand, and leads him out of the circle,—he is not treated as an offender, only he does not choose to do as the others do, therefore he is not wanted there: the next time, he is quite content to be a frog. Here we have the principle for the discipline of the nursery. Do not treat the child's small contumacy too seriously; do not assume that he is being naughty: just leave him out when he is not prepared to act in harmony with the rest. Avoid friction; and above all, do not let him disturb the moral atmosphere; in all gentleness and serenity, remove him from the company of the others, when he is being what nurses call 'tiresome.'

"Once more, the Kindergarten professes to take account of the joyousness of the child's nature: to allow him full and free expression for the glee that is in him, without the 'rampaging' which follows if he is left to himself to find an outlet for his exuberant life. This union of joy and gentleness is the very temper to be cultivated in the nursery. The boisterous behaviour sometimes allowed in children is unnecessary—within doors, at any rate: but even a momentary absence of sunshine on the faces of her children will be a graver cause of uneasiness to the mother" (Vol. 1, pp. 180, 181).

9. The child is a person and should be respected as an individual, not treated as just another plant in the garden.

"The true *Kindergartnerin* is the artist amongst teachers; she is filled with the inspiration of her work, and probably most sincere teachers have caught something from her fervour, some sense of the beauty of childhood, and of the enthralling delight of truly educational work.

"And yet I enter a *caveat*. Our first care should be to preserve the individuality, to give play to the personality, of children. Now *persons* do not grow in a garden, much less in a greenhouse. It is a doubtful boon to a person to have conditions too carefully adapted to his needs. The exactly due sunshine and shade, pruning and training, are good for a plant whose uses are subordinate, so to say, to the needs and pleasures of its owner. But a *person* has other uses in the world, and mother or teacher who regards him as a plant and herself as the gardener, will only be saved from grave mistakes by the force of human nature in herself and in her child.

"The notion of supplementing Nature from the cradle is a dangerous one. A little guiding, a little restraining, much reverent watching, Nature asks of us; but beyond that, it is the wisdom of parents to leave children as much as may be to Nature, and 'to a higher Power than Nature itself' " (Vol. 1, p. 186).

"The world suffered that morning when the happy name of 'Kindergarten' suggested itself to the greatest among educational 'Fathers.' No doubt it was

Notes

A caveat *is a caution or warning.*

Notes

simple and fit in its first intention as meaning an out-of-door garden life for the children; but, a false analogy has hampered, or killed, more than one philosophic system—the child became a plant in a well-ordered garden. The analogy appealed to the orderly, scientific German mind, which does not much approve of irregular, spontaneous movement in any sort. Culture, due stimulus, sweetness and light, became the chief features of a great educational code. From the potting-shed to the frame and thence to the flower-bed, the little plant gets in due proportion what is good for him. He grows in a seemly way, in ordered ranks; and in fit season puts forth his flower.

"Now, to figure a *person* by any analogy whatsoever is dangerous and misleading; there is nothing in nature commensurable with a person. Because the analogy of the garden plant is very attractive, it is the more misleading; manifestations of purpose in a plant are wonderful and delightful, but in a person such manifestations are simply normal. The outcome of any thought is necessarily moulded by that thought, and to have a cultivated garden as the ground-plan of our educational thought, either means nothing at all, which it would be wronging the Master to suppose, or it means undue interference with the spontaneous development of a human being" (Vol. 1, pp. 189, 190).

"It is questionable whether the conception of children as cherished plants in a cultured garden has not in it an element of weakness. Are the children too carefully tended? Is Nature too sedulously assisted? Is the environment too perfectly tempered? Is it conceivable that the rough-and-tumble of a nursery should lend itself more to the dignity and self-dependence of the *person* and to the evolution of individual character, than that delightful place, a child-garden? I suppose we have all noticed that children show more keen intelligence and more independent thought in home-play and home-talk than one expects of the angelic little beings one sees at school" (Vol. 3, pp. 56, 57).

" 'Make children happy and they will be good,' is absolutely true, but does it develop that strenuousness, the first condition of virtue, which comes of the contrary axiom—'Be good and you will be happy'? Kindergarten teachers are doing beautiful work; but many of them are hampered by the original metaphor of the *plant*, which is exactly lacking in that element of personality, the cherishing and developing of which is a sacred and important part of education" (Vol. 3, p. 57).

10. Adults must be careful not to undervalue a child's intelligence by the books and activities they give him.

"The promoters of the kindergarten system have done much to introduce games of this, or rather of a more educational kind; but is it not a fact that the singing games of the kindergarten are apt to be somewhat inane? Also, it is doubtful how far the prettiest plays, learnt at school and from a teacher, will take hold of the children as do the games which have been passed on from hand to hand through an endless chain of children, and are not be found in the print-books at all" (Vol. 1, p. 82).

"Those of us who have watched an urchin of seven making Catherine-wheels down the length of a street, or a group of little girls dancing to a barrel organ, or small boys and girls on a door-step giving what Dickens calls 'dry nourishment' to their babies, or a small girl sent by her mother to make four careful purchases out of sixpence and bring home the change—are not ready to believe that physical, mental, and moral development waits, so to speak, upon Kindergarten teaching. Indeed, I am inclined to question whether, in the interest of carrying out a system, the charming Kindergartnerin is not in danger sometimes of greatly undervaluing the intelligence of her children. I know a person of three who happened to be found by a caller alone in the drawing-room. It was spring, and the caller thought to make himself entertaining with talk about the pretty 'baa-lambs.' But a pair of big blue eyes were fixed upon him and a solemn person made this solemn remark, "Isn't it a dwefful howid thing to see a pig killed!" We hope she had never seen or even heard of the killing of a pig, but she made as effective a protest against twaddle as would any woman of Society. Boers and kopjes, Russians and Japs, Treasure Island, Robinson Crusoe and his man Friday, the fight of Thermopylae, Ulysses and the Suitors—these are the sorts of things that children play at by the month together; even the toddlers of three and four will hold their own manfully with their brothers and sisters. And, if the little people were in the habit of telling how they feel, we should learn perhaps that they are a good deal bored by the nice little games in which they frisk like lambs, flap their fins, and twiddle their fingers like butterflies" (Vol. 1, pp. 186, 187).

11. Though children might enjoy being humored, they are capable of greater thoughts than twaddle.

" 'But,' says the reader, 'children do all these things so pleasantly and happily in the Kindergarten!' It is a curious thing about human nature that we all like to be managed by persons who take the pains to play on our amiabilities. Even a dog can be made foolishly sentimental; and, if we who are older have our foibles in this kind, it is little wonder that children can be wooed to do anything by persons whose approaches to them are always charming. It is true that 'W. V.,' the child whom the world has been taught to love, sang her Kindergarten songs with little hands waving in the 'air so blue'! but that was for the delectation and delusion of the elders when bedtime came. 'W. V.' had greater thoughts at other times" (Vol. 1, pp. 187, 188).

12. Most teachers interfere too much by excessively directing, expecting, and suggesting.

"There are still, probably, Kindergartens where a great deal of twaddle is talked in song and story, where the teacher conceives that to make poems for the children herself and to compose tunes for their singing and to draw pictures for their admiration, is to fulfil her function to the uttermost. The children might echo Wordsworth's complaint of 'the world,' and say, the teacher is too much with us, late and soon. Everything is directed, expected, suggested. No other personality out of book, picture, or song, no, not even that of Nature herself, can get at the children without the mediation of the teacher. No room is left for spontaneity or personal initiation on their part" (Vol. 1, p. 188).

13. A teacher with a magnetic personality may cause a child to learn only for the sake of pleasing his teacher rather than for the joy of learning itself.

"Most of us are misled by our virtues, and the entire zeal and enthusiasm of the

---

Notes

"Twaddle" refers to books that underestimate a child's intelligence, that talk down to him in diluted words.

Notes

Mother-games were "very crude poems, indifferent music and pictures, illustrating certain incidents of child life believed to be of fundamental and typical significance" (Vol. 1, p. 198).

Kindergartnerin is perhaps her stone of stumbling. 'But the children are so happy and good!' Precisely; the home-nursery is by no means such a scene of peace, but I venture to think it a better growing-place. I am delighted to see that an eminent Froebelian protests against the element of personal magnetism in the teacher; but there is, or has been, a good deal of this element in the successful Kindergartner, and we all know how we lose vigour and individuality under this sort of influence. Even apart from this element of charm, I doubt if the self-adjusting property of life in the Kindergarten is good for children" (Vol. 1, pp. 188, 189).

14. Organized, systematic games and activities between a mother and her baby or toddler are not natural.

"To begin with the 'Mother-games,' a sweet conception, most lovingly worked out. But let us consider; the infant is exquisitely aware of every mood of his mother, the little face clouds with grief or beams with joy in response to the expression of hers. The two left to themselves have rare games. He jumps and pulls, crows and chuckles, crawls and kicks and gurgles with joy; and, amid all the play, is taught what he may *not* do. Hands and feet, legs and arms, fingers and toes, are continually going while he is awake; mouth, eyes and ears are agog. All is play without intention, and mother plays with baby as glad as he. Nature sits quietly by and sees to it that all the play is really work; and development of every sort is going on at a greater rate during the first two years of life than at any like period of after life—enough development and not too much, for baby is an inordinate sleeper. Then comes in the educator and offers a little more. The new games are so pretty and taking that baby might as well be doing these as his own meaningless and clumsy jumpings and pattings. But a real labour is being put upon the child in addition to the heaviest two years' work that his life will know. His sympathy with his mother is so acute that he perceives something strenuous in the new play, notwithstanding all the smiles and pretty talk; he answers by endeavour, great in proportion as he is small. His nerve centres and brain power have been unduly taxed, some of the joy of living has been taken from him, and though his baby response to direct education is very charming, he has less latent power left for the future calls of life" (Vol. 1, pp. 190, 191).

15. True socialization occurs in the company of mixed ages rather than in an isolated group of children all the same age.

"Let us follow the little person to the Kindergarten, where he has the stimulus of classmates of his own age. It certainly is stimulating. For ourselves, no society is so much so as that of a number of persons of our own age and standing; this is the great joy of college life; a wholesome joy for all young people for a limited time. But persons of twenty have, or should have, some command over their inhibitory centres. They should not permit the dissipation of nerve power caused by too much social stimulus; yet even persons of twenty are not always equal to the task of self-management in exciting circumstances. What then, is to be expected of persons of two, three, four, five? That the little person looks rather stolid than otherwise is no guarantee against excitement within. The clash and sparkle of our equals now and then stirs us up to health; but for everyday life, the mixed society of elders, juniors and equals, which we get in a family, gives at the same time the most repose and the most room for individual development. We have all wondered at the good sense, reasonableness, fun and resourcefulness shown by a child in his own home as compared with the same child in school life" (Vol. 1, p. 191).

16. Too much organization and structure can hinder a child's development; children need lots of free play.

"Danger lurks in the Kindergarten, just in proportion to the completeness and beauty of its organisation. It is possible to supplement Nature so skilfully that we run some risk of supplanting her, depriving her of space and time to do her own work in her own way. 'Go and see what Tommy is doing and tell him he mustn't,' is not sound doctrine. Tommy should be free to do what he likes with his limbs and his mind through all the hours of the day when he is not sitting up nicely at meals. He should run and jump, leap and tumble, lie on his face watching a worm, or on his back watching the bees in a lime tree. Nature will look after him and give him promptings of desire *to know* many things; and somebody must tell as he wants to know; and *to do* many things, and somebody should be handy just to put him in the way; and *to be* many things, naughty and good, and somebody should give direction" (Vol. 1, pp. 191, 192).

17. A good deal of letting alone helps a child develop personal initiative.

"Here we come to the real crux of the Kindergarten question. The busy mother says she has no leisure to be that somebody, and the child will run wild and get into bad habits; but we must not make a fetish of habit; education is a *life* as well as a discipline. Health, strength, and agility, bright eyes and alert movements, come of a free life, out-of-doors, if it may be; and as for habits, there is no habit or power so useful to man or woman as that of personal initiative. The resourcefulness which will enable a family of children to invent their own games and occupations through the length of a summer's day is worth more in after life than a good deal of knowledge about cubes and hexagons, and this comes, not of continual intervention on the mother's part, but of much masterly inactivity" (Vol. 1, p. 192).

"We all admire spontaneity, but this grace, even in children, is not an indigenous wild-flower. In so far as it is a grace, it is the result of training,—of pleasant talks upon the general principles of conduct, and wise 'letting alone' as to the practice of these principles" (Vol. 3, p. 43).

18. A parent's job is to sow opportunities for the child and then keep in the background.

"The educational error of our day is that we believe too much in mediators. Now, Nature is her own mediator, undertakes, herself, to find work for eyes and ears, taste and touch; she will prick the brain with problems and the heart with feelings; and the part of mother or teacher in the early years (indeed, all through life) is to sow opportunities, and then to keep in the background, ready with a guiding or restraining hand only when these are badly wanted. Mothers shirk their work and put it, as they would say, into better hands than their own, because they do not recognise that wise letting alone is the chief thing asked of them, seeing that every mother has in Nature an all-sufficient handmaid, who arranges for due work and due rest of mind, muscles, and senses" (Vol. 1, pp. 192, 193).

Notes

For more on the concepts of "masterly inactivity" and "wise letting alone", download the free e-book, **Masterly Inactivity,** *at http://SimplyCharlotteMason.com*

Notes

19. A child given plenty of free play and plenty of opportunities for learning at his own pace in a natural home environment will be prepared for formal lessons by the time he is six or seven.

"In one way the children of the poor have better chances than those of the rich. Poor children get education out of household ways; but there is a great deal of teaching to be got out of a wisely ordered nursery, and their own small persons and possessions should, as I have said, afford much 'Kindergarten' training to the little family at home. At six or seven, definite lessons should begin, and these need not be watered down or served with jam for the acute intelligences that will in this way be brought to bear on them" (Vol. 1, p. 193).

20. An only child would probably be better off playing with a friend than attending a structured Kindergarten.

"But what of only children, or the child too old to play with her baby brother? Surely the Kindergarten is a great boon for these! Perhaps so; but a cottage-child as a companion, or a lively young nursemaid, might be better" (Vol. 1, p. 193).

21. A child who has plenty of free time and is surrounded by opportunities to learn in a natural environment will teach himself as he is ready.

"A child will have taught himself to paint, paste, cut paper, knit, weave, hammer and saw, make lovely things in clay and sand, build castles with his bricks; possibly, too, will have taught himself to read, write, and do sums, besides acquiring no end of knowledge and notions about the world he lives in, by the time he is six or seven. What I contend for is that he shall do these things because he chooses (provided that the standard of perfection in his small works be kept before him)" (Vol. 1, pp. 193, 194).

22. Other than the regular routine of family life, a child should be given freedom to order his play.

"The details of family living will give him the repose of an ordered life; but, for the rest, he should have more free-growing time than is possible in the most charming school. The fact that lessons look like play is no recommendation: they just want the freedom of play and the sense of his own ordering that belongs to play. Most of us have little enough opportunity for the ordering of our own lives, so it is well to make much of the years that can be given to children to gain this joyous experience" (Vol. 1, p. 194).

23. A child left to himself will think more and better.

"Miss Sullivan had little love for psychologists and all their ways; would have no experiments; would not have her pupil treated as a phenomenon, but as a person. 'No,' she says, 'I don't want any more Kindergarten materials. . . . I am beginning to suspect all elaborate and special systems of education. They seem to me to be built up on the supposition that every child is a kind of idiot who must be taught to think, whereas if the child is left to himself he will think more and better, if less showily. Let him go and come freely, let him touch real things, and combine his impressions for himself, instead of sitting indoors at a little round table, while a sweet-voiced teacher suggests that he build a stone wall with his wooden blocks,

Anne Sullivan was Helen Keller's teacher.

or make a rainbow out of strips of coloured paper, plant straw trees in bead flowerpots. Such teaching fills the mind with artificial associations that must be got rid of before the child can develop independent ideas out of actual experiences' " (Vol. 1, pp. 195, 196).

Notes

Notes

Beginning Reading

Though Charlotte advocated teaching reading when a child turned six, we include her beginning reading lessons so you can see what activities will lay a solid foundation before actual reading lessons. We also realize that some children are ready, even eager, to learn to read before they turn six years old. Since you know your child much better than anyone else does, use this section in a way that will be best for your child.

1. Recognize that different children are ready to read at different ages.

"*Reading* presents itself first amongst the *lessons* to be used as instruments of education, although it is open to discussion whether the child should acquire the art unconsciously, from his infancy upwards, or whether the effort should be deferred until he is, say, six or seven, and then made with vigour" (Vol. 1, p. 199).

"They begin their 'schooling' in 'letters' at six, and begin at the same time to learn mechanical reading and writing. . . .

"But children are not all alike; there is as much difference between them as between men or women; two or three months ago, a small boy, not quite six, came to school (by post); and his record was that he could read anything in five languages, and was now teaching himself the Greek characters" (Vol. 6, pp. 30, 31).

2. Many children teach themselves to read, so don't let the idea of teaching reading intimidate you.

"Many persons consider that to learn to read a language so full of anomalies and difficulties as our own is a task which should not be imposed too soon on the childish mind. But, as a matter of fact, few of us can recollect how or when we learned to read: for all we know, it came by nature, like the art of running; and not only so, but often mothers of the educated classes do not know how their children learned to read. 'Oh, he taught himself,' is all the account his mother can give of little Dick's proficiency. Whereby it is plain, that this notion of the extreme difficulty of learning to read is begotten by the elders rather than by the children" (Vol. 1, p. 200).

3. At the same time, recognize that learning to read does require effort, so do all you can to make the task easy and inviting.

"Probably that vague whole which we call 'Education' offers no more difficult and repellent task than that to which every little child is (or ought to be) set down—the task of learning to read. We realise the labour of it when some grown man makes a heroic effort to remedy shameful ignorance, but we forget how contrary to Nature it is for a little child to occupy himself with dreary hieroglyphics—all so dreadfully alike!—when the world is teeming with interesting objects which he is agog to know. But we cannot excuse our volatile Tommy, nor is it good for him that we should. It is quite necessary he should know how to read; and not only so—the discipline of the task is altogether wholesome for the little man. At the same time, let us recognise that learning to read is to many children hard work, and let us do what we can to make the task easy and inviting" (Vol. 1, p. 214).

4. Use a combination of sight words and phonics to teach reading.

"Definitely, what is it we propose in teaching a child to read? (a) that he shall know at sight, say, some thousand words; (b) That he shall be able to build up new words with the elements of these. Let him learn ten new words a day, and in twenty weeks he will be to some extent able to read, without any question as to the number of letters in a word. For the second, and less important, part of our task, the child must know the sounds of the letters, and acquire power to throw given sounds into new combinations" (Vol. 1, pp. 215, 216).

Preparation for Reading

1. Make a game of putting together the words in word families.

"Exercises treated as a game, which yet teach the powers of the letters, will be better to begin with than actual sentences. Take up two of his letters and make the syllable 'at': tell him it is the word we use when we say 'at home,' 'at school.' Then put *b* to 'at'—*bat*; *c* to 'at'—*cat; fat, hat, mat, sat, rat,* and so on" (Vol. 1, p. 202).

2. Use actual words and let the child say and make each one with its initial consonant added.

"First, let the child say what the word becomes with each initial consonant; then let him add the right consonant to 'at,' in order to make *hat, pat, cat*. Let the syllables all be actual words which he knows. Set the words in a row, and let him read them off" (Vol. 1, p. 202).

3. Continue the process with other short-vowel three-letter words.

"Do this with the short vowel sounds in combination with each of the consonants, and the child will learn to read off dozens of words of three letters, and will master the short-vowel sounds with initial and final consonants without effort. Before long he will do the lesson for himself. 'How many words can you make with "en" and another letter, with "od" and another letter?' etc." (Vol. 1, p. 202).

4. Do not hurry your child.

"Do not hurry him" (Vol. 1, p. 202).

5. After he has mastered short-vowel three-letter words, teach the silent-e that makes a long vowel in the word in the same way.

"When this sort of exercise becomes so easy that it is no longer interesting, let the long sounds of the vowels be learnt in the same way: use the same syllables as before with a final *e*; thus 'at' becomes 'ate,' and we get *late, pate, rate*, etc. The child may be told that *a* in 'rate' is *long a*; *a* in 'rat' is *short a*. He will make the new sets of words with much facility, helped by the experience he gained in the former lessons" (Vol. 1, pp. 202, 203).

See chapter 12 for ideas on teaching the alphabet and the letters' sounds.

Notes

6. Continue the process with consonant combinations, like "ng" and "th."

"Then the same sort of thing with final 'ng'—'ing,' 'ang,' 'ong,' 'ung'; as in *ring, fang, long, sung*: initial 'th,' as *then, that*: final 'th,' as *with, pith, hath, lath*, and so on, through endless combinations which will suggest themselves" (Vol. 1, p. 203).

7. These word games are not reading, but they lay the foundation for future reading lessons.

"This is not reading, but it is preparing the ground for reading; words will be no longer unfamiliar, perplexing objects, when the child meets with them in a line of print" (Vol. 1, p. 203).

8. Encourage your child to pronounce correctly any word that he learns.

"Require him to pronounce the words he makes with such finish and distinctness that he can himself hear and count the sounds in a given word" (Vol. 1, p. 203).

9. Encourage him to shut his eyes and spell the word he has made, thus preparing him for future spelling lessons.

"Accustom him from the first to shut his eyes and spell the word he has made. This is important. Reading is not spelling, nor is it necessary to spell in order to read well; but the good speller is the child whose eye is quick enough to take in the letters which compose it, in the act of reading off a word; and this is a habit to be acquired from the first: *accustom* him to *see* the letters in the word, and he will do so without effort.

"If words were always made on a given pattern in English, if the same letters always represented the same sounds, learning to read would be an easy matter; for the child would soon acquire the few elements of which all words would, in that case, be composed. But many of our English words are, each, a law unto itself: there is nothing for it, but the child must learn to know them at sight; he must recognise 'which,' precisely as he recognises '*B*,' because he has seen it before, been made to look at it with interest, so that the pattern of the word is stamped on his retentive brain. This process should go on side by side with the other—the learning of the powers of the letters; for the more variety you can throw into his reading lessons, the more will the child enjoy them. Lessons in word-making help him to take intelligent interest in *words*; but his progress in the art of reading depends chiefly on the 'reading at sight' lessons" (Vol. 1, pp. 203, 204).

Reading Lessons Guidelines

1. Proceed slowly, making sure your child has mastered a concept before moving on to the next.

"The teacher must be content to proceed very slowly, securing the ground under her feet as she goes" (Vol. 1, p. 204).

2. Read aloud a short portion of a children's poem or prose, pointing to each word as you say it.

"Say—
 'Twinkle, twinkle, little star,
 How I wonder what you are,'
is the first lesson; just those two lines. Read the passage for the child, very slowly, sweetly, with just expression, so that it is pleasant to him to listen. Point to each word as you read" (Vol. 1, p. 204).

3. Point to the words out of order and have your child say each with careful enunciation.

"Then point to 'twinkle,' 'wonder,' 'star,' 'what,'—and expect the child to pronounce each word in the verse taken promiscuously" (Vol. 1, p. 204).

"The little people will probably have to be pulled up on the score of pronunciation. They must render 'high,' 'sky,' 'like,' 'world,' with delicate precision; 'diamond,' they will no doubt wish to hurry over, and say as 'di'mond,' just as they will reduce 'history' to 'hist'ry.' But here is another advantage of slow and steady progress—the *saying* of each word receives due attention, and the child is trained in the habit of careful enunciation" (Vol. 1, p. 206).

4. When he shows that he knows each word by itself, let him read the two lines with good enunciation and expression.

"Then, when he shows that he knows each word by itself, and not before, let him *read* the two lines with clear enunciation and expression: insist from the first on clear, beautiful reading, and do not let the child fall into a dreary monotone, no more pleasant to himself than to his listener. Of course, by this time he is able to say the two lines; and let him say them clearly and beautifully. In his after lessons he will learn the rest of the little poem" (Vol. 1, p. 204).

"A beautiful word deserves to be beautifully said, with a certain roundness of tone and precision of utterance. Quite young children are open to this sort of teaching, conveyed, not in a lesson, but by a word now and then" (Vol. 1, p. 227).

5. Have your child identify on a few pages of printed type the words he has learned.

"The child should hunt through two or three pages of good clear type for 'little,' 'star,' 'you,' 'are,' each of the words he has learned, until the word he knows looks out upon him like the face of a friend in a crowd of strangers, and he is able to pounce upon it anywhere. Lest he grow weary of the search, the teacher should guide him, unawares, to the line or paragraph where the word he wants occurs. Already the child has accumulated a little capital; he knows eight or ten words so well that he will recognise them anywhere, and the lesson has occupied probably ten minutes" (Vol. 1, p. 205).

6. Begin the next lesson by reviewing familiar words in printed type first, then repeat the process described above with the next lines of the poem or passage.

Notes

Notes

"The next 'reading at sight' lesson will begin with a hunt for the familiar words, and then—

'Up above the world so high,
Like a diamond in the sky,'

should be gone through in the same way" (Vol. 1, p. 205).

7. Encourage him to recite the poems and passages that he has learned as he masters each.

"At this stage, his reading lessons must advance so slowly that he may just as well learn his reading exercises, both prose and poetry, as recitation lessons. Little poems suitable to be learned in this way will suggest themselves at once; but perhaps prose is better, on the whole, as offering more of the words in everyday use, of Saxon origin, and of anomalous spelling" (Vol. 1, pp. 204, 205).

8. Use good poetry and prose even at this stage, not twaddle.

"Even for their earliest reading lessons, it is unnecessary to put twaddle into the hands of children" (Vol. 1, p. 205).

"When there is so much noble poetry within a child's compass, the pity of it, that he should be allowed to learn twaddle!" (Vol. 1, p. 226).

9. Randomly ask your child to spell one of the shorter words he has learned. Do not make him study it, but ask periodically to encourage him to cultivate the habit of looking at how words are spelled.

"As spelling is simply the art of *seeing*, seeing the letters in a word as we see the features of a face—say to the child, 'Can you spell sky?'—or any of the shorter words. He is put on his mettle, and if he fail this time, be sure he will be able to spell the word when you ask him next; but do not let him *learn* to spell or even say the letters aloud with the word before him" (Vol. 1, pp. 205, 206).

10. Don't worry about reading comprehension; your child will understand what he reads in his lesson if you use this method.

"As for understanding what they read, the children will be full of bright, intelligent remarks and questions, and will take this part of the lesson into their own hands; indeed, the teacher will have to be on her guard not to let them carry her away from the subject" (Vol. 1, p. 206).

11. Keep the reading lesson short and gradually lengthen it as your child knows more words.

"Reading lessons must be short; ten minutes or a quarter of an hour of fixed attention is enough for children of the ages we have in view" (Vol. 1, p. 230).

"Every day increases the number of words he is able to read at sight, and the more words he knows already, the longer his reading lesson becomes in order to afford the ten or a dozen new words which he should master every day" (Vol. 1, p. 206).

"Twaddle" refers to books that underestimate a child's intelligence, that talk down to him in diluted words.

12. Using this method, your child will learn 2,000–3,000 words in a year.

" 'But what a snail's progress!' you are inclined to say. Not so slow, after all: a child will thus learn, without appreciable labour, from two to three thousand words in the course of a year; in other words, he will learn *to read*, for the mastery of this number of words will carry him with comfort through most of the books that fall in his way" (Vol. 1, p. 206).

13. Focus on setting up good habits of reading and reading with care.

"The child who has been taught to read with care and deliberation until he has mastered the words of a limited vocabulary, usually does the rest for himself. The attention of his teachers should be fixed on two points—that he acquires the *habit* of reading, and that he does not fall into *slipshod habits* of reading" (Vol. 1, p. 226).

Two Mothers' Conversation about Teaching Reading

(Vol. 1, pp. 207–214)

"You don't mean to say you would go plump into words of three or four syllables before a child knows his letters?"

"It is possible to read words without knowing the alphabet, as you know a face without singling out its features; but we learn not only the names but the *sounds* of the letters before we begin to read words."

"Our children learn their letters without any teaching. We always keep by us a shallow table drawer, the bottom covered half an inch deep with sand. Before they are two, the babies make round *O* and crooked *S*, and *T* for Tommy, and so on, with dumpy, uncertain little fingers. The elder children teach the little ones by way of a game."

"The sand is capital! We have various devices, but none so good as that. Children love to be doing. The funny, shaky lines the little finger makes in the sand will be ten times as interesting as the shapes the eye sees."

"But the reading! I can't get over three syllables for the first lesson. Why, it's like teaching a twelve-months old child to waltz!"

"You say that because we forget that a group of letters is no more than the *sign* of a word, while a word is only the vocal sign of a thing or an act. This is how the child learns. First, he gets the notion of the table; he sees several tables; he finds they have legs, by which you can scramble up; very often covers which you may pull off; and on them many things lie, good and pleasant for a baby to enjoy; sometimes, too, you can pull these things off the table, and they go down with a bang, which is nice. The grown-up people call this pleasant thing, full of many interests, 'table,' and, by-and-by, baby says 'table' too; and the word 'table' comes to mean, in a vague way, all this to him. 'A round table,' 'on the table,' and so on, form part of the idea of 'table' to him. In the same way baby chimes in when his mother sings. She says, 'Baby, sing,' and, by-and-by, notions of 'sing,' 'kiss,' 'love,' dawn on his brain."

"Yes, the darlings! and it's surprising how many words a child knows even before

Appendix

Notes

he can speak them; 'pussy,' 'dolly,' 'carriage,' soon convey interesting ideas to him."

"That's just it. Interest the child in the thing, and he soon learns the *sound-sign* for it—that is, its name. Now, I maintain that, when he is a little older, he should learn the *form-sign*—that is, the printed word—on the same principle. It is far easier for a child to read plum-pudding than to read 'to, to,' because 'plum-pudding' conveys a far more interesting idea."

"That may be, when he gets into words of three or four syllables; but what would you do while he's in words of one syllable—indeed, of two or three letters?"

"I should never put him into words of one syllable at all. The bigger the word, the more striking the look of it, and, therefore, the easier it is to read, provided always that the idea it conveys is interesting to a child. It is sad to see an intelligent child toiling over a reading-lesson infinitely below his capacity—*ath, eth, ith, oth, uth*—or, at the very best, 'The cat sat on the mat.' How should we like to begin to read German, for example, by toiling over all conceivable combinations of letters, arranged on no principle but similarity of sound; or, worse still, that our readings should be graduated according to the number of letters each word contains? We should be lost in a hopeless fog before a page of words of three letters, all drearily like one another, with no distinctive features for the eye to seize upon; but the child? 'Oh, well—children are different; no doubt it is good for the child to grind in this mill!' But this is only one of many ways in which children are needlessly and cruelly oppressed!"

"You are taking high moral ground! All the same, I don't think I am convinced. It is far easier for a child to spell c a t, cat, than to spell p l u m - p u d d i n g, plum-pudding."

"But spelling and reading are *two* things. You must learn to spell in order to *write* words, not to *read* them. A child is droning over a reading-lesson, spells c o u g h; you say 'cough,' and she repeats. By dint of repetition, she learns at last to associate the look of the word with the sound, and says 'cough' without spelling it; and you think she has arrived at 'cough' through c o u g h. Not a bit of it; c o f spells cough!"

"Yes; but 'cough' has a silent *u*, and a *gh* with the sound of *f*. There, I grant, is a great difficulty. If only there were no silent letters, and if all letters had always the same sound, we should, indeed, have reading made easy. The phonetic people have something to say for themselves."

"You would agree with the writer of an article in a number of a leading review: 'Plough ought to be written and printed *plow*; through, *thru*; enough, *enuf*; ought, *aut* or *ort*'; and so on. All this goes on the mistaken idea that in reading we look at the letters which compose a word, think of their sounds, combine these, and form the word. We do nothing of the kind; we accept a word, written or printed, simply as the *symbol* of a word we are accustomed to say. If the word is new to us we may try to make something of the letters, but we know so well that this is a shot in the dark, that we are careful not to *say* the new word until we have heard someone else say it."

"Yes, but children are different."

"Children are the same, 'only more so.' *We* could, if we liked, break up a word into its sounds, or put certain sounds together to make a word. But these are efforts beyond the range of children. First, as last, they learn to know a word by the look of it, and the more striking it looks the easier it is to recognise; provided always that the printed word is one which they already know very well by sound and by sense."

"It is not clear yet; suppose you tell me, step by step, how you would give your first reading lesson. An illustration helps one so much."

"Very well: Bobbie had his first lesson yesterday—on his sixth birthday. The lesson was part of the celebration. By the way, I think it's rather a good idea to begin a new study with a child on his birthday, or some great day; he *begins* by thinking the new study a privilege."

"That is a hint. But go on; did Bobbie know his letters?"

"Yes, he had picked them up, as you say; but I had been careful not to allow any small readings. You know how Susanna Wesley used to retire to her room with the child who was to have his first reading-lesson, and not to appear again for some hours, when the boy came out able to read a good part of the first chapter of Genesis? Well, Bobbie's first reading-lesson was a solemn occasion, too, for which we had been preparing for a week or two. First, I bought a dozen penny copies of the 'History of Cock Robin'—good bold type, bad pictures, that we cut out.

"Then we had a nursery pasting day—pasting the sheets on common drawing-paper, six one side down, and six the other; so that now we had six complete copies, and not twelve.

"Then we cut up the *first page only*, of all six copies, line by line, and word by word. We gathered up the words and put them in a box, and our preparations were complete.

"Now for the lesson. Bobbie and I are shut in by ourselves in the morning-room. I always use a black-board in teaching the children. I write up, in good clear 'print' hand,

    C o c k R o b i n

Bobbie watches with more interest because he knows his letters. I say, pointing to the word, 'cock robin,' which he repeats.

"Then the words in the box are scattered on the table, and he finds half a dozen 'cock robins' with great ease.

"We do the same thing with 'sparrow,' 'arrow,' 'said,' 'killed,' 'who,' and so on, till all the words in the verse have been learned. The words on the black-board grow into a column, which Bob reads backwards and forwards, and every way, except as the words run in the verse.

"Then Bobbie arranges the loose words into columns like that on the board.

"Then into columns of his own devising, which he reads off.

"Lastly, culminating joy (the whole lesson has been a delight!), he finds among the loose words, at my dictation,

    'Who killed Cock Robin
    I said the sparrow
    With my bow and arrow
    I killed Cock Robin,'

arranging the words in verse form.

"Then I had still one unmutilated copy, out of which Bob had the pleasure of reading the verse, and he read it forwards and *backwards*. So long as he lives he will know those twelve words."

"No doubt it was a pleasant lesson; but, think of all the pasting and cutting!"

"Yes, that is troublesome. I wish some publisher would provide us with what we want—nursery rhymes, in good bold type, with boxes of loose words to match,—a separate box, or division, for each page, so that the child may not be confused by having too many words to hunt amongst. The point is that he should *see*, and *look at*, the new word many times, so that its shape becomes impressed on his brain."

"I see; but he is only able to read 'Cock Robin'; he has no general power of reading."

"On the contrary, he will read those twelve words wherever he meets with them. Suppose he learns ten words a day, in half a year he will have at least six hundred words; he will know how to read a little."

"Excellent, supposing your children *remember* all they learn. At the end of a week, mine would remember 'Cock Robin,' perhaps, but the rest would be gone!"

"Oh, but we keep what we get! When we have mastered the words of the second verse, Bob runs through the first in the book, naming words here and there as I point to them. It takes less than a minute, and the ground is secured."

"The first lesson must have been long?"

"I'm sorry to say it lasted half an hour. The child's interest tempted me to do more than I should."

"It all sounds very attractive—a sort of game—but I cannot be satisfied that a child should learn to read without knowing the powers of the letters. You constantly see a child spell a word over to himself, and then pronounce it; the more so, if he has been carefully taught the sounds of the letters—not merely their names."

"Naturally; for though many of our English words are each a law unto itself, others offer a key to a whole group, as arrow gives us sp arrow, m arrow, h arrow; but we have alternate days—one for reading, the other for word-building—and that is one way to secure variety, and, so, the joyous interest which is the real secret of success."

Some Beginning Reading Lesson Plans

(from Vol. 1 pp. 217–222)

Day 1

Background: The child knows his letters by name and sound, but he knows no more.

Objective: To-day he is to be launched into the very middle of reading, without any "steps" at all, because reading is neither an art nor a science, and has, probably, no beginning. Your child is to learn to read to-day—

"I like little pussy,

Her coat is so warm"—

and he is to know those nine words so well that he will be able to read them wherever they may occur henceforth and for evermore.

Materials Needed
- Box of loose letters
- First two lines of the poem "Little Pussy" typed in large print on seven sheets of paper; six of the sheets should be cut into separate words

- Chalkboard and chalk, paper and pencil, or whiteboard and dry-erase marker

Lesson

Step 1: Write "Pussy" on the chalkboard, paper, or whiteboard in a large print and tell your child this word is "pussy."

Step 2: Tell your child to look at the word until he is sure he would know it again.

Step 3: Have your child make "pussy" from memory with his own loose letters.

Step 4: Scatter the individual word slips on the table and have your child find all that say "pussy."

Step 5: Show him the printed sheet with the first two lines of the poem, and have him find "pussy." (Don't tell him the rhyme yet.)

Step 6: Teach each of the remaining words, out of order, following the same steps. As each new word is added, have your child make a column of the already-learned word slips. He may rearrange this column as often as he likes and read the words. Also review your list on the chalkboard, paper, or whiteboard in random order as new words are added.

Step 7: Once all the words have been learned individually, ask your child to find the correct word strips in order as you say them. Make a short sentence using the words he knows. For example, "Pussy—is—warm." Have your child place the word strips in "reading" order and read the sentence.

Step 8: Continue making new sentences with the words he knows. For example, "her—little—coat—is—warm," "Pussy—is—so—little," "I—like—pussy," "Pussy—is—little—like—her—coat." If the rhyme can be kept secret until the end, so much the better.

Day 2

Background: The child knows the nine words from yesterday's poem lines.

Objective: Introduce new words by using word families.
Coat, boat, goat, float, moat, stoat
Little, brittle, tittle, skittle
Like, Mike, pike
So, no, do (the musical "do"), lo
Warm, arm, harm, charm, barm, alarm

Materials Needed
- Box of loose letters
- Word slips from the first two lines of the poem "Little Pussy" (used on Day 1)
- Chalkboard and chalk, paper and pencil, or whiteboard and dry-erase marker
- Tokens or pennies

Lesson

Step 1: Have your child make the word "coat" with his letters—from memory if he can; if not, looking at the word slip for a pattern.

Step 2: Pronounce the word slowly, then give the initial consonant sound *C*.

Notes

Your child should not begin to read until he is equal to the effort required by these lessons. Even then, it may be well to break up one lesson into two, or half a dozen, as he is able to take it.

"I Like Little Pussy"
by Jane Taylor

I like little Pussy,
Her coat is so warm;
And if I don't hurt her
She'll do me no harm.
So I'll not pull her tail,
Nor drive her away,
But Pussy and I
Very gently will play.
She shall sit by my side,
And I'll give her some food;
And she'll love me because
I am gentle and good.

I'll pat little Pussy,
And then she will purr;
And thus show her thanks
For my kindness to her.
I'll not pinch her ears,
Nor tread on her paw,
Lest I should provoke her
To use her sharp claw;
I never will vex her,
Nor make her displeased,
For Pussy can't bear
To be worried or teased.

Appendix

Notes

If your child suggests a word that sounds like the word family you're working on but is spelled differently, simply explain that that word is spelled another way and move on.

Pronounce "warm" as "arm." Your child will probably perceive that such a pronunciation is wrong and notice that all these words are sounded like "arm," but not one of them like "warm"—that is, he will see that the same group of letters need not always have the same sound. But do not ask him to make a note of this new piece of knowledge; let it grow into him gradually, after many experiences.

Step 3: Say, "Take away *C*, and what do we have left?" With a little help, he will figure out "oat."

Step 4: Ask, How would you make boat?" (saying the word slowly and emphasizing the sound of *B)*. Write "boat" on the chalkboard or whiteboard and have your child make it with his letters.

Step 5: Continue making new words in that word family by changing the initial consonant. Give brief explanations of any words that are unfamiliar to him.

Step 6: Review the new words in random order as you proceed.

Step 7: Dictate short sentences that use the already-learned words and the new words, and have your child locate and place the words in the correct "reading" order. Use the word slips for the old words and have your child make the new words with his loose letters. For example, "I—like—her—goat," "Her—little—stoat—is—warm."

Step 8: Give a sentence that contains a word or two that your child hasn't learned yet. For example, "Pussy—is—in—the—boat." Have your child put tokens or pennies where the unknown words belong in the sentence with the promise that "they may soon come up in our lessons."

Step 9: Deal with the remaining word families in the same way. Sample sentences: "Her skittle is little," "Her charm is brittle," "Her arm is warm." Take care that the sentences make sense.

Step 10: Have your child write his new words in a notebook.

Day 3

Do the next two lines of the poem in the same manner as Day 1.

Day 4

Learn new words by word families (as on Day 2) based on the words learned on Day 3. Or, if the words learned on the previous day do not offer much in the way of word families, use this day to move on to the next two lines of the poem.

"Our stock of words is growing; we are able, as we go on, to make an almost unlimited number of little sentences. If we have to use counters now and then, why, that only whets our appetite for knowledge. By the time Tommy has worked 'Little Pussy' through he has quite a large stock of words; has considerable power to attack new words with familiar combinations; what is more, he has achieved; he has courage to attack all 'learning,' and has a sense that delightful results are quite within reach. Moreover, he learns to read in a way that affords him some moral training. There is no stumbling, no hesitation from the first, but bright attention and perfect achievement. His reading lesson is a delight, of which he is deprived when he comes to his lesson in a lazy, drawling mood. Perfect enunciation and precision are insisted on, and when he comes to arrange the whole of the little rhyme in his loose words and read it off (most delightful of all the lessons) his reading must be a perfect and finished recitation" (Vol. 1, pp. 221, 222).

Math

Charlotte did not discuss any kind of mathematics to be done in the early years. However, if you want to include some kind of mathematical instruction, here are some basic principles to keep in mind from her discussion of math lessons for school-age children.

1. Keep the math concepts within the child's grasp.

"Engage the child upon little problems within his comprehension from the first" (Vol. 1, p. 254).

2. Use objects to demonstrate concepts.

"The next point is to demonstrate everything demonstrable" (Vol. 1, p. 255).

"A bag of beans, counters, or buttons should be used in all the early arithmetic lessons, and the child should be able to work with these freely" (Vol. 1, p. 256).

"Let him learn 'weights and measures' by measuring and weighing" (Vol. 1, p. 260).

3. Let the child learn numbers and mathematical concepts naturally.

"I do not think that any direct preparation for mathematics is desirable. The child, who has been allowed to think and not compelled to cram, hails the new study with delight when the due time for it arrives" (Vol. 1, p. 264).

Notes

In Charlotte's day, "direct preparation" meant continually showing the child pictures of shapes and numerals. "In the 'forties' and 'fifties' it was currently held that the continual sight of the outward and visible signs (geometrical forms and figures) should beget the inward and spiritual grace of mathematical genius, or, at any rate, of an inclination to mathematics" (Vol. 1, p. 263).

Notes

Writing

Charlotte did not teach handwriting until the child was six years old. However, if your child exhibits an interest in learning to write before he is six, here are some basic principles from Charlotte's writing lessons for school-age children.

1. Encourage your child to give his best effort.

"First, let the child accomplish something *perfectly* in every lesson—a stroke, a pothook, a letter" (Vol. 1, p. 233).

"The thing to be avoided is the habit of careless work—humpy *m*'s, angular *o*'s" (Vol. 1, p. 234).

2. Keep writing lessons short: 5–10 minutes maximum.

"Let the writing lesson be short; it should not last more than five or ten minutes. Ease in writing comes by practice; but that must be secured later" (Vol. 1, pp. 233, 234).

3. Start with simple uppercase letters that have single curves and straight lines. When he can make all the uppercase letters, move to lowercase, but allow your child to write them large.

"First, let him print the simplest of the capital letters with single curves and straight lines. When he can make the capitals and large letters, with some firmness and decision, he might go on to the smaller letters—'printed' as in the type we call '*italics*,' only upright,—as simple as possible, and large" (Vol. 1, p. 234).

4. Group letters with similar angles and strokes together.

"Let the stroke be learned first; then the pothook; then the letters of which the pothook is an element—*n, m, v, w, r, h, p, y*; then *o*, and letters of which the curve is an element—*a, c, g, e, x, s, q*; then looped and irregular letters—*b, l, f, t*, etc. One letter should be perfectly formed in a day, and the next day the same elemental forms repeated in another letter, until they become familiar" (Vol. 1, p. 234).

5. As soon as possible, group known letters into words.

"By-and-by copies, three or four of the letters they have learned grouped into a word—'man,' 'aunt'; the lesson to be the production of the written word *once* without a single fault in any letter" (Vol. 1, p. 234).

6. Do early writing on a chalkboard or whiteboard rather than on paper.

"At this stage the chalk and blackboard are better than pen and paper, as it is